SIEGFRIED

and ROY

with Annette Tapert

MASTERING THE IMPOSSIBLE

William Morrow and Company, Inc.
New York

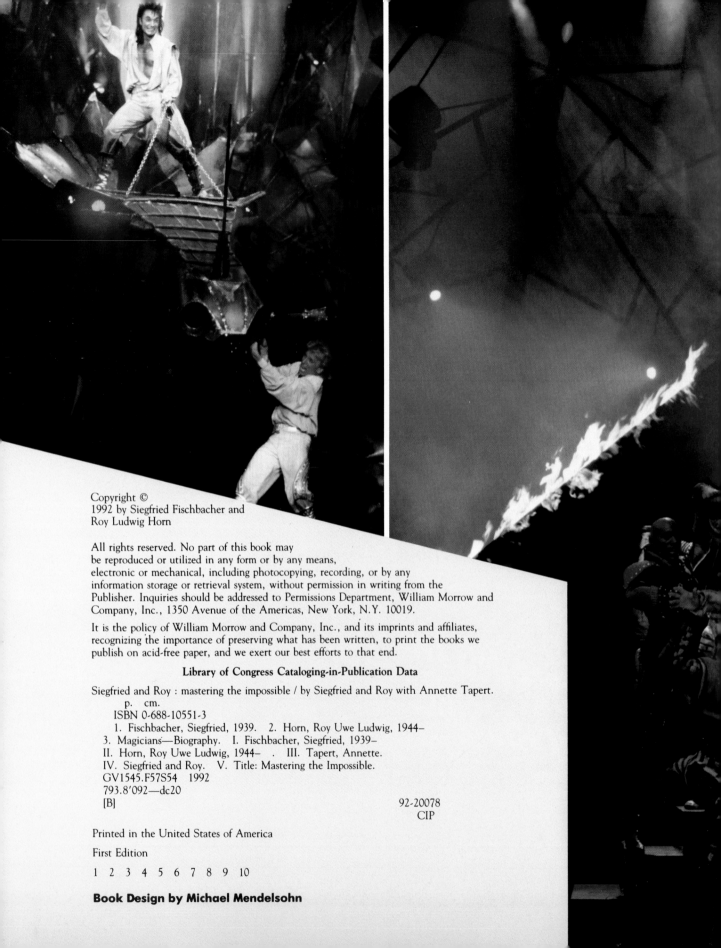

It is the policy of William Morrow and Company, Inc., and its imprints and affiliates,
recognizing the importance of preserving what has been written, to print the books we
publish on acid-free paper, and we exert our best efforts to that end.

Library of Congress Cataloging-in-Publication Data

Siegfried and Roy : mastering the impossible / by Siegfried and Roy with Annette Tapert.
    p.   cm.
  ISBN 0-688-10551-3
    1. Fischbacher, Siegfried, 1939.   2. Horn, Roy Uwe Ludwig, 1944–
3. Magicians—Biography.   I. Fischbacher, Siegfried, 1939–
II. Horn, Roy Uwe Ludwig, 1944–   .   III. Tapert, Annette.
IV. Siegfried and Roy.   V. Title: Mastering the Impossible.
GV1545.F57S54   1992
793.8'092—dc20
[B]   92-20078
                                                   CIP

Printed in the United States of America

First Edition

1 2 3 4 5 6 7 8 9 10

Book Design by Michael Mendelsohn

TNT

Contents

Prologue

It took a great deal of courage to write this book.

The first rule of magic is that a magician never tells his secrets. We are respectful of our profession, and we would never do that. But what was the alternative: a celebrity scrapbook, with an unbroken stream of anecdotes that reveals everyone's character except our own?

Well, there was the true story. And that terrified us. If we wrote honestly about our lives—which began with difficulty and great unhappiness—would we destroy the fantasy and effortlessness that magic requires? Could we bear to share stories that we had never told anyone and, in some instances, had never even told each other? How would our audience regard such revelations?

It was when we began to delve into our childhoods that we understood there was a powerful link between our reality and our magic, for our reality, even at its darkest, turns out to be the source of our magic. By strength, will, and determination, we rose from unwholesome environments in our native Germany. We followed our dreams, for dreams were all we had. In the process our lives became magical.

Today we read so much about the dramas of childhood that it seems miraculous anyone becomes a successful adult. We identify with those who struggle against demons—child abuse, alcoholism, divorce, dysfunctional families, poverty. But we don't view any of these tragic situations as excuses for defeat or explanations for despair. And so we write not as masters of illusion but as masters of human possibility.

That philosophy propels us to write a book that is far from the one we had envisioned; we fervently believe that no matter where you come from or how hard your life is, you have the power to take your fantasies and make them real. It takes belief and effort and honesty. And, of course, courage.

Welcome, Bienvenue, Wilkommen

ACT ONE

Within all of us there is an elusive melody which when heard and followed leads to the fulfillment of our fondest dreams.

Siegfried

Day after day, as I walked home from school in the years after the war ended, I looked in the shop windows at the few luxuries a young boy would dream about—sweets and pastries. I could never afford them. But I never passed those shops without looking in.

One afternoon, when I was eight, my eye was caught by something in the window of the bookstore, a book on magic. More than forty years later I can't explain what drew me to this book, but when I look back on it, there must have been an unaccountable force involved. I went in, asked to see it, and studied it far more intently than any school subject. It didn't take long for me to conclude that I had to have this book.

All that stood in my way was the money to pay for it. Five marks. For me a fortune. A fortune for any little boy in Germany in 1947. But I was determined to own it.

My only hope was to earn the money. So I went home, and I was the nicest kid you could ever imagine. My behavior was completely out of character. I cleaned my room; I set the dinner table; I washed the dishes. My mother, who was the eldest of eight children and knew every trick there was, immediately understood I was up to something.

Siegfried

Halfway through the dishwashing, she stood over me and said, "What's the matter with you?"

"Well, there is this magic book—"

I got no further. "What? A magic book? You must be out of your mind," she screeched. And she threw up her hands and walked out of the kitchen.

"Please," I called, hurrying after her, "it's only five marks, please can I have it?"

"Five marks! You know that's impossible."

I knew it was, but I still kicked and cried in hope that my pleading would make her give in. And of course, nothing worked.

We lived on the outskirts of Rosenheim, quite a distance from the shops. It wasn't the right time to go shopping, I certainly had no money to spend, but without knowing what I was doing, I left the house and walked to town. I'd never felt such strength, such certainty—and I've never felt it quite so strongly since. For this was my first experience with determination, with wanting something and knowing I was destined to have it. I didn't know how I was going to get that book, but I knew it was going to be mine.

Now what happened next sounds like a fairy tale, but it's true, and maybe in a funny way this was my first real experience with magic. I was across the street from the bookstore, balancing myself on the curb of the sidewalk like a tightrope artist and at the same time trying to figure out what to do next, when I looked down. There lying on the pavement was five marks. You know what I did with it.

I made my way back home, walking and reading at the same time, knowing full well that to explain this to my mother, who was not a great believer in fairy tales or miracles, would be difficult. But now that I had the book, I didn't care about anything else. I could face any punishment.

Confidently I opened the door. My mother was waiting. She saw the book—and slapped me harder than I've ever been slapped, before or since. Of course, she *knew* I stole it. The more I tried to tell her of the incredible event that had allowed me to buy the book, the less she believed me.

I don't remember what further punishment ensued, if any, because the only important fact was that I had the book. I went silently to my bedroom, and I began to study it. I studied it, and studied it, and studied it—at night, after school, at every free moment. Cards, coins, disappearing balls: I practiced until I had memorized the directions.

There was one trick I did particularly well right from the start. You have a coin, a handkerchief, and a glass of water; you drop the coin in the glass, and it vanishes. It was my first expression of mastery, and naturally, I showed it to my parents. My father just looked at me with astonishment and said, "How did you do that?"

A reasonable response in most homes, but for me, his praise was like magic in itself, for in a home where children were brought up in the strict Bavarian way, it was the first time my father ever acknowledged me. Until that moment I didn't really exist for him; I went to school, came home, ate, went out to play, and then it was bedtime. Now not only had my father spoken to me, but his astonishment suggested I had done something he couldn't—a remarkable moment for a boy trained to believe his father knew everything.

And that was the beginning of magic for me.

Roy

When I was a little boy, my favorite pastime was to roam the open fields that surrounded Nordenham, my hometown in northern Germany. Ours was a region of stark scenic beauty, made up of long, flat stretches of coastal plain situated against a backdrop of gentle, low, rolling grass-covered hills, heaths, woodland, and huge marshland. I loved this marshland. Hexe, my dog, loved it too. She was jet-black and half wolf. Together we were explorers. Or I was a prince, and Hexe was my unicorn. We ran, we flew, we knew no boundaries. We were a team, and we were free.

One June morning when I was six, I woke up and decided it was too glorious a day to go to school. I gath-

Roy in the fields of northern Germany with his mother and Hexe

ered up Hexe, and off we went. That morning our adventure began with the sighting of a dark, velvety mole that had come up out of its hole. We chased it, but it disappeared belowground.

We romped and roamed, and then, under an old willow, I fell asleep. The next thing I knew, I was opening my eyes. I thought I heard a voice. Hexe was gone. Where was she? I stood up to look for her and saw, instead, a black raven staring at me with dark, cunning eyes. I remembered that someone told me that ravens will steal anything that is gold or silver or has a shine.

I was fascinated by the behavior of the bird as it walked and fluttered in front of me and seemed to talk to me in what sounded like the crackling voice of an old woman. I slowly followed the raven, and each time I stopped it would stop, too; I'd make a move and it would do the same. I continued my game until it eventually passed by another old willow tree with the branches hanging down to the grass and disappeared behind a clump of tall reeds. I followed, thinking that behind that grass there must be a nest where the bird was hiding all its treasures.

I was quite anxious to get over to where the raven was, and as I climbed over the high reeds, I fell forward and instantly felt myself sink. I tried to raise my feet to walk, but they wouldn't budge. I pushed harder, but still nothing moved. Next, I tried to crawl, but that didn't work either. I started to scream for help at the top of my lungs, but the more I did that, the deeper I sank.

Now I was really frightened. I frantically waved my arms about, pulling up on the tall reeds all around me in hope that they might lift me up. Meanwhile, the raven was standing on firm ground, cackling so hard that it sounded like vicious laughter. The bird seemed quite delighted that it had lured me into the swamp.

But now Hexe appeared, howling. The raven flew away. Though Hexe knew I was in danger, there was nothing she could do to help me without endangering herself. When she disappeared again, I was terrified even more. Had my best friend deserted me?

By now I was up to my chest in wetland. Crying, begging, and praying, I cried out, "Hexe, Hexe, help me, help me," until I had almost no voice left. Then I heard voices, real voices. A farmer came into my sight with Hexe right beside him. "Good Lord," he called out, "hang on, boy."

He ran away, leaving me alone again for what seemed like an endless time but was probably only a few minutes. The farmer returned with another man and a rope, which they threw to me, again and again, until it finally landed over my head and arms. They pulled for what seemed forever until at last the swamp lost its hold on me and the two old men were able to pull me to safety.

I was crying and shaking all over, thanking the farmers through my tears, but they insisted that I should really thank my animal. Apparently the men were working in the fields when Hexe came running and jumped around them. They didn't know what to make of her but decided to follow her. Soon enough, they heard my screams and knew what was happening.

When the farmer said that, I fell to my knees and hugged my Hexe for dear life, pressing my little face against hers while she licked away my tears. This was not the first time, nor would it be the last, that I would be thankful to one of my animals for my safety or that the harmony I felt with an animal would be the strongest—and most magical—connection in my life.

This is, I think, the key to understanding that despite all our apparent differences, Siegfried and I are alike. In magic he found a way to escape the unhappy atmosphere of his homelife and receive the attention from other people that he never got from his parents. For me the escape route from a childhood seen through silent tears to solace and peace was through animals. Curious, isn't it? At opposite ends of our country, we both found our reason to believe.

Siegfried

When your passport says "Born: Germany, 1939," it's like letting the world know you were born on the darker side of life. Before I was two, my father was sent to fight with Hitler's army in Russia and eventually became a prisoner of war. My mother, like almost every other German wife at the time, spent the next four years caring for my brother, sister, and me under impossible circumstances.

To say it plainly, we had nothing. My mother's saving grace—and this was true for all women in her position—was that everyone in our village pulled together and helped one another. In that sense, maybe we were luckier during the war than after, because when the war ended, it was assumed that private life would begin

Siegfried posing in his lederhosen

again. For those families with no men coming home, grief and hardship became more bitter. And for many families, like mine, that had fathers who returned, it was as if they brought the war home with them.

For when my father returned from Russia, he was an alcoholic. He was able to reestablish his house-painting business, but he could never build it back up to what it had been. It was my mother who had to hold it together. So we struggled, financially and emotionally. Looking back, I realize she must have done a good job with the business for we were the first family in our village to have a telephone and a few other modern conveniences.

Perhaps my mother could have changed the situation, but for her, divorce was not an option. She was a traditional Catholic housewife, brought up to believe that you marry, have children, and accept your lot in life, good or bad.

So my mother resigned herself to a joyless life. As a result, it was hard for her to show any emotion other than distress and dissatisfaction. With so much discontent all around, it is no wonder that she couldn't show positive emotion or outwardly display the love that I know she had in her heart for her children. I never saw my parents kiss or hug each other or us. I never heard them say, "*Ich liebe dich.*" In turn, we never hugged our parents or said we loved them.

As it is for any child who grows up with an alcoholic parent, my childhood was made up of many dramas, yet it's not the specific events that stand out for me; it's the feelings. And it is those feelings that made me develop into what I am today. Looking at a magic act, you may think magicians are the most confident of people. To present the manipulations, it's true, we have to be, but like entertainers and actors, a magician is often born from insecurity, lack of

Siegfried (*right*), **brother Marinus** (*left*), **and sister Margot under the wings of their mother, Maria**

attention, and the need to be loved. For me, magic was not only a vehicle to get recognition but also a way to escape the unpleasant atmosphere of my homelife. Of all the things it gave me, the first and most important was solace.

Once I had the magic book, I was always practicing—and happy. I walked to school on my own with my right hand playing cards and my left making coins disappear. Well, not real coins. I always used a button. If I'd had a coin, I would have bought candy.

Sometimes I got carried away with my newfound hobby, and that led to problems. After my initial success at home, I mastered another vanishing coin trick. In this one, you grab someone behind the ears and produce a coin and then you vanish it. I decided to try it out on my friends.

So on my way to school one day I performed it for my schoolmates. My movements had become as smooth as glass, and I got just the right reaction from the other kids. As soon as I finished, my friend Otto, who was a real prankster and often my partner in crime, spied an elderly lady coming toward us and suggested it would be fun if I performed my brilliant manipulation on a stranger. Otto and I ran up to her and grabbed her. Then I took my button and made it reappear and disappear. The woman became hysterical; she was certain we had taken a button off her coat. And despite our protests, she told the principal of the school that Otto and I had stolen her button.

In those days children were always wrong, no questions asked. We were sent straight away to the cellar and locked in. Unfortunately the teacher forgot about us. Two, three, four hours passed, and no one came. By this time poor Otto had to go to the bathroom. He was afraid to relieve himself on the floor—that might have meant further punishment—so he looked around for another solution. As it happened, there were some barrels of sauerkraut in the cellar. With tears running down his face and doubled over in pain from having held it for so long, he climbed up on the barrel, pushed the sauerkraut aside, as a cat does in its litter box. Then, at last, he unloaded his business in the sauerkraut. And once again, like a cat, when he finished, he covered it up. Through the window we saw it get dark out; everyone had forgotten us. Thank God for the maintenance man, who arrived at dinnertime and let us out.

Three things came out of that experience: No one was ever sent to the cellar again, I never ate sauerkraut again, and I never, ever performed another magic trick with buttons.

One thing that incident didn't do: keep me away from magic. For magic is something that once it gets into your blood, it's like nothing else. It becomes your mistress, and you become obsessed.

I remember that when I was no more than twelve, I was performing some magic for a few people, and I overheard someone say there was a magic store in Munich. I was cut off in many ways from the rest of the world, and I had never even considered there would be such a thing as a shop for magic. We had a Munich phone book, so the first thing I did when I got home was look up the store. And there it was, *"Der Zauberkönig"* ("The king of magic").

The only problem was that Munich was about thirty miles from Rosenheim. My mother would never have dreamed of letting me go to the big city by myself. Even if I had been able to persuade her, once she found out I was going for magic, never. My only solution was to ride my father's bicycle there. I got up before sunrise one morning, made myself some sandwiches, and rode off without anyone's knowing.

Getting there was no easy task. My father's bike was way too big for me. My feet couldn't touch the pedals, so I had to ride, not on the seat but crouched down, one leg between the crossbar to reach the other pedal. If you had seen me, you would have said this was no budding magician but a contortionist in training.

I finally arrived in the afternoon, with only the address and not a clue to where the shop might be. Many wrong turns later I found the magic shop. For the longest time I just stared into the window. I couldn't believe what lay before me. It was everything I had dreamed: feathers, flowers, silks, canes, all the things I longed to know about. Finally I got up the courage to walk in. The lady working behind the counter must have been between eighty and death, an old, withered, and wrinkled Hungarian Gypsy woman with sunken cheeks, a scarf around her head, and huge hoop earrings. In the most polite way I could think of, I asked her if she could show me some magic.

"What kind do you want to see?"

I looked around. What caught my eye was a small box that looked as if you could pull out silks forever. Very politely I asked to see the box, but neither my manners nor my schoolboy innocence endeared me to her.

"How much money do you have?" she snapped.

"None," I said. "But if you could show me how the box works—"

"This is only for professional magicians," she said in a harsh, nasty tone that assured me there was no way she would ever show me that box without first seeing a fistful of bills.

I walked out of the store and glumly rode all the way back to Rosenheim. It didn't, however, bother me that I had traveled so far for nothing. My curiosity and my desire to experience things were so great that I figured if you wanted to do something badly enough, you found a way. Nothing could stop me.

I think I was born with this set of charactersics—self-motivation, determination, ambition—for there was no one in my life giving me the confidence that is often needed to make these traits blossom and flourish. Everything in life was viewed with negativity;

in Rosenheim the glass was always half empty. Not just in my home, it seemed to be true of everyone, from the neighbor lady on down to the shopkeeper, to the egg man. Reality was all there was, and you just made the best of it. Dreams, fantasies, and ambitions were reserved for the rest of the world.

I quickly outgrew the few tricks in my little magic book. But learning more was a problem. In Germany at that time magic was a very secretive craft. You saw it in the traveling carnivals, performed by circus people and Gypsies who weren't about to share the secrets of their meager livelihood with an enthusiastic boy. So I learned to develop things on my own, using the only resources I had—my instinct and imagination.

Siegfried—anything for attention!

I taught myself how to eat light bulbs and swallow razor blades. Not as those tricks are done in a magic show, but the Siegfried Fischbacher way, which was *really* to eat them. With a lot of thought and practice I figured out a way to digest them so I wouldn't do more damage to myself than cut and scar my tongue. Looking back, I realize how crazy I was; though I was simply finding a way to create my own magic, I was also using magic to impress my audience, my friends. I wanted to do something they wouldn't dare in order to gain their respect and acceptance.

I lived for the summer, when the traveling carnivals passed through Rosenheim and I could watch the magicians perform and then try to duplicate their tricks. On one occasion my friends and I went to a carnival where the magician claimed he could eat razor blades. To prove they were authentic, he asked someone to come up from the audience and check them out. Well, as you can imagine, I was dying to get up there, so I jumped up and walked onstage. I studied the blades very carefully. No doubt about it, they were real. And then, because I loved being on any stage and seeing all my friends looking up at me, I very dramatically ate every last razor blade myself.

Everyone in the audience started to scream. The performers were so furious they wanted to beat me off the stage. Meanwhile, my friends were cheering me on. And me, I was delighted to know I was the talk of the town.

Still, this story is a metaphor for how I've always gone about my magic and illusions. Even after I met Roy, we never got anything out of reading a book or having someone show us how to do it. My illusions have always been something I created and figured out for myself.

I wasn't always successful. When I was fourteen, I put on a magic show that was a disaster. It was at a club of goat farmers, and I was doing fine right up to the climax, when I wanted to make a goat disappear. Well, the goat vanished, but the twinkling tail didn't. I tried and tried, but I couldn't vanish the tail. The goat farmers thought it was hilarious, but for the moment, at least, I gave up all hope of ever making large animals disappear.

And there were times when my magic wasn't just an escape—it was something I could use to change unhappy situations. One of the features of Bavarian life is that the man gets his weekly wages on Friday, hits the beer halls that night, and drinks with his buddies. In our case, however, my father was always at the local tavern. He had bought himself a car and had several accidents while driving intoxicated. My brother and I would have to go collect him, bruised and bloody, and bring him home. As we carried him up to the door, my poor mother would be waiting, sick with worry that he had killed himself.

One time, when I was about fourteen, he went out on a binge and didn't come home. For three long days, my mother cried and cried, "This time, I know he'll get killed if he drives himself home." Finally, I could stand it no longer. I wanted to ease her pain, so I went to the tavern.

How was I going to get the key so he couldn't use the car? I knew it was useless to ask him outright. There he was, talking and drinking with his buddies—all of them drunk.

At first, he thought my mother had sent me. I sat with him for a while. Once I sensed that he was no longer suspicious of my presence, I jovially announced I wanted to show him and his pals some magic. I asked the owner for a piece of rope, I casually asked my father for his car key, tied it on the string, placed a handkerchief over it, quickly and artfully pulled it off—and the key vanished. And as I left them amazed, I vanished myself.

If I had known the consequences my ingenious stroke of magic would bring, I might not have done it. As soon as I left, I had a bad feeling about what I had done. Sooner or later, he was going to realize I had outsmarted him, and because of that, he would look like a fool in front of his friends. I knew I was doomed. So when I arrived home, I went straight to bed and pretended I was asleep.

My father came home not too long after that. I lay frozen, my heart thumping as I heard him barge through the house. A few minutes later, he broke through my bedroom door. He was like a man possessed. Then I saw the sturdy rubber hose in his hand. He charged toward me and beat me and beat me and when he wasn't sure if I'd had enough, he beat me some more. He would have beaten me to death if my brother hadn't arrived to protect me.

And yet I was able to forgive my father, for I realized he was not himself—he was under the influence, and his alcoholism was really an illness. It was a painful lesson, but a good one. Never again would I use magic at the expense of someone else; it was only for entertainment and pure wonderment.

Roy

I've heard the story of my wartime birth so many times from my mother that although I can't have remembered it, it absolutely feels as if I saw it all. October 3, 1944—and Johanna Horn had the misfortune to be nine months pregnant. Just at that point, Allied bombings began to light up Bremerhaven and the neighboring city of Nordenham—both major defense ports—like a blood-red torch. Houses were burning; women and children were screaming. Everyone who wasn't buried under rubble or confident of the family's basement shelter rushed to the Weser, the river where there were small boats and the comparative safety of water.

Roy, age two—Ready to roll with the punches

In her basement in Nordenham Johanna Horn didn't know what to do. On one hand, there were three small children to protect and comfort. On the other, there was a life coming, for in the middle of all this insanity, she was going into labor.

Johanna voted with the future. Telling her children not to leave the basement, she climbed on her bicycle and desperately pedaled across the city. Bombs burst around her, but she reached the safety of her sister's home unharmed. Fifteen minutes later she gave birth to the last of four sons. Her dreams, faith, and destiny—sprinkled with hope—were placed in a little crib.

And that, family legend has it, is how Roy Uwe Ludwig Horn was born.

The chances of any infant's surviving the final year of the war weren't good. There wasn't much food. And there was even less fuel that long, cold winter. My mother took to breaking little pieces of ice-covered wood off the picket fence in the hope that the tiny fire she made would keep us alive.

This was the unhappy situation my father returned to after years of fighting on the Russian front. Before the war he'd been a successful orchestra leader who took pleasure in teaching his sons any of the six instruments he played. After 1945, like Siegfried's father, he was not the same man; he was fighting a private war. Unlike Siegfried's parents, mine divorced soon after the war ended; although I spent time with my father after that, we never really established a bond, and I eventually stopped visiting him.

Soon after her divorce my mother married a man who had also returned from the war. At the time she didn't know of his emotional turmoil and could not foresee the mental anguish he ultimately put our family through. Things started well: I had a nanny, there were lavish birthday parties, and, best of all, my stepfather treated me like his own son. It was by all accounts a privileged existence.

Though I had three brothers, I was, in a way, like an only child. Alfred, the eldest son, had already left home. Werner lived with our real father, and Manfred, though old enough to be on his own, stayed with us intermittently because of a motorcycle accident that left him riddled with medical problems. He was operated on many times and would come to convalesce with our mother. However, I never felt as if I were the favorite child. As I perceived it, Alfred, though the black sheep, was the most loved; Manfred, because of his illness, was the most dependent on my mother; and Werner, who shared the same birthday as Johanna, was closest to her heart. Myself, I got what was left.

My stepfather, a highly intelligent and successful man, managed a large construction company and, unlike many at the time, was in a business that was flourishing in postwar Germany. My mother, who had been struggling since the beginning of the war, felt that she had, at last, found some security. All might have continued to go well, except that my stepfather was cursed with leg injuries left over from the war, thrombosis, and, to a certain degree, some mental injuries.

Because he was by nature a strong man who couldn't tolerate weakness in himself, he turned to alcohol to alleviate his pain. As time went by and his pain increased, so did his drinking. The loving man who showered his wife and stepson with adoration and

**Roy off to experience his first
day of school**

presents soon gave way to a domineering, jealous, possessive tyrant fixated on the fear of losing the only people who mattered to him: my mother and me.

Eventually his mental and physical deterioration made it impossible for him to work. Because he had been a tremendous asset to his company, he was awarded a pension that was to make his life comfortable. Unfortunately the war had torn apart the bureaucratic system. Company records housed in buildings that had been bombed during the war were lost, and so it took not months but years before he was able to receive this income. We were able to live on his savings for a short while, but once those dried up and the pension still had not come through, we had to go on welfare to survive.

When it was time for me to start school, my mother went to work to make sure I would have proper clothes like the other children. In the worst winter weather she rose at five-thirty in the morning and loaded her rickety old bicycle onto the ferryboat that crossed the Weser River to Bremerhaven. Once there, she cycled for miles to reach the factory where she worked for twelve hours. These long hours made it impossible for her to send me off to school or be there when I returned home—a terrible penalty for a woman whose only ambition in life was to be a wife and mother.

This situation forced me to become self-reliant. Barely over kindergarten age, I got myself up in the morning, made my own breakfast, took myself to school, and came home alone. And then, in order to avoid the alcoholic rantings and ravings of my stepfather, I sneaked down to the cellar, crawled out of the window, and escaped with Hexe to roam the fields until my mother came home. Not surprisingly, I was lonely and alienated, and my Hexe became not just my escape but my only friend.

In the evening the dramas only increased. A day's drinking intensified my stepfather's irrational feelings, and by dinnertime they reached such a pitch that the nights became a living hell for my mother and me. My stepfather threatened us with rat poison he kept in the kitchen cabinet and the ax he hid in the china closet. I had discovered the ax

Roy, flirting with the camera and showing off his new bicycle—the first boy in his village to have one

one day but never dreamed he'd use it. Then, one night, he took it out. My mother and I fled to my room and locked ourselves in, while my stepfather drunkenly cursed us and tried to chop through the thick wooden door. This went on for hours—and not just on that night—while my mother and I huddled together.

Yes, we could have called for help. We still lived in the compound that was owned

by the company my stepfather had worked for, and there was a night watchman who patrolled the premises every hour. But my mother was reluctant to speak up, and I understood her reluctance: The last thing she wanted was to provoke my stepfather. So we were in a sense his prisoners, which is exactly what he wanted us to be.

My stepfather could easily have broken the lock on my bedroom door, but it was only because of my wolf that he wasn't able to enter. In effect, Hexe became our guard. And that intensified my relationship with her; she was the only creature I could totally trust. Each night, when the nightmare finally ceased, I cried myself to sleep on her chest.

It is said the intelligence of an animal can never be what ours is, because what makes human beings superior is that we have complex thoughts and animals don't. I learned very early that animals sense my thoughts before I have them. People who don't have strong attachments to animals may feel this is mushy mysticism; for me it is simply a fact.

And so, when people ask, as they often do, how I developed such harmony with my animals, I rarely give a complete answer. I've never told anyone except Siegfried the full story of my childhood. And I'm shy about describing my relationship with animals as a living karma, as a destiny, as the sum of my aura.

How can I explain to well-meaning strangers that it's because of what I experienced as a child that my security— my certainty of unconditional trust, unconditional emotion, and unconditional strength—comes from my animals? Would it be interpreted correctly if I admitted that my animals and I are like partners in crime? Who could understand that no matter what happens between me and the people I care about, the real love affair in my life will always be with my animals? Although it's hard to discuss, the reality of my life is very simple. My animals are the friends who will accept me always for what I am—rich or poor, fat or thin, dumb or intelligent.

Siegfried

Magic was not the only thing in my life when I was growing up. I was interested in everything connected to performing—from magic to theater. This was largely because I was under the influence of Father Johann, the priest in my village.

At that time in Germany the priest was one of the most important people in any community. And during the war Father Johann had played a crucial role in the lives of the children of Rosenheim; he replaced many fathers. For me he was a permanent replacement. Not only did he hold my family together, but he was my mentor; he gave me a window to look through that held a little light. For I was his special case.

Father Johann was a frustrated actor, and he built a small stage in his backyard so the village children could perform plays. When he saw that I adored performing and was good at it, he began to nurture my talent and groom me to become an actor.

I loved playing different characters, and when I got to be about fifteen, I developed a stand-up comedy act. I performed on weekends at weddings, parties, and town functions. As my routines lampooned the dry humor of my fellow Bavarians and poked fun at some of our local characters, I soon became a minor celebrity in Rosenheim.

In order to play as many as five different characters of varying ages, I had to learn how to use makeup. I fooled everyone; I could

Siegfried as an altar boy assisting Father Johann, the priest in his village. Like many Bavarian Catholic boys, he had considered becoming a priest.

Siegfried's first attempt to take command of the stage

look as old as I needed to. This created a problem after the show, when people in the audience invited their entertainer to sit and have a drink with them. Without my makeup I was just this young boy—and they were disappointed. So from the moment I walked offstage I was my usual insecure self. To make up for this inadequacy, I would no sooner sit at a table than I'd start doing magic. And then everybody, including me, would have a great time.

It was actually Father Johann who took me to my first real magic show. It was to see Kalanag, the great German illusionist, perform in Munich. This was the highlight of my childhood and, to this day, one of the most exciting events in my life, for Kalanag stimulated and inspired me to become a magician. It wasn't just his illusions that thrilled me; it was his personality and the glamour of the elaborate stage sets. I saw for the first time that with charm and style a magician could color the illusions. Magic, I realized, is only 50 percent dexterity. You practice, practice, practice until the moves are in your blood and you don't have to think about them anymore; it's like learning a language. When you're at that point, the magic becomes a part of you, and you start all over again, injecting your personality into your act.

Kalanag merged magic and personality brilliantly. Seeing him, I realized that my desire to perform onstage as an actor and my passion for magic could be put together.

R*oy*

I was a hopeless schoolboy. After a long night of family dramas I dragged myself out of bed, so tired I could hardly keep my eyes open. I dozed through school and came home groggy, too tired to do my homework. Another boy might have worried that he was falling behind. I turned into a dreamer and a fantasist.

One incident illustrates my school career in a nutshell. For homework we were to write a story about the sea—supposedly an easy assignment, because we lived surrounded by water. After a hopeless night I had prepared nothing. And the teacher was going down the aisle, asking us to read our stories out loud. I prayed the class would end before he called on me, but no luck. I stood, looked down at the blank page on my desk, and, with a gulp, began.

"The little fishing boat cut with difficulty through the stormy sea, with dark clouds in the sky, the sea-foam whipping across the deck. The storm turned to ice and hail, and the crew realized they must turn back. The youngest crew member was dragging in the heavy net when suddenly a cry echoed across the boat. The boy had been washed overboard. The crew ran to the railing. They saw nothing. Then, yes, a little head and an arm stretched toward the clouds, a prayer for help. Then came the large ice floes, and he was seen no more. 'Uwe, Uwe, where are you?' cried the crew. And when the boat finally made it back to the dock, there was the boy's mother waiting, arms out, repeating the same question."

As I told this story, I came to believe it. I gave quite a performance. I didn't realize that the class was silent and the teacher was standing right next to me. Unfortunately for me, he was looking down. What had led him to my desk wasn't my great reading but the fact that I never turned the page. He pulled me to the front of the room by my ear and sent me off to the principal's office.

Here, for once, there was a happy ending. The principal liked fantasy. He had me write the story down—for real. And then he sent it, as an example, to some of the other classes.

My flights into fantasy were healthy defense mechanisms for me because at the core of this undernourished shrimp of a boy there was a full-blown optimist with a genuine love of life. Despite everything, I believed there was something better beyond my world. And so I made up stories, flew into other dimensions, drowned myself in books, roamed the fields with my animals, and played pretend toreador with the bulls that grazed on the meadows of the marsh. Somewhere, I was confident, I would see the true colors of life.

My optimism was so total that other people regarded me as a lovable child with a sunny disposition. And regardless of what was going on, I was basically a happy boy. No one saw me cry; that I reserved for the moments when I was alone with Hexe. With people around, you could beat me and I wouldn't shed a tear; you could never punish me enough to beat me down. In some ways that toughness was useful. In others it wasn't; this strength and will agitated my stepfather and made him determined to break my spirit. Thank God he never could, because aside from my animal that was all I had.

Yes, there were people around me I could have turned to for help. I had two grandmothers, a real father, an eldest brother who was by now an adult. But pride and shame kept me from doing anything. I wanted to protect my mother and whatever was left of our little circle. I didn't want relatives or friends to know what was going on.

So no matter how bad it was, I never complained. And believe me, there were many days when we didn't have enough to eat and I was really starving, days when I looked out from the snow-encrusted window of our house and saw my stepfather, passed out on a child's sleigh, being dragged up to the front door by strangers.

Fortunately there was a big, bright spot in my life—my mother's best friend and her husband. They were childless, and they adored me. Though "Aunt Paula" had to know what was going on at home, she never pushed me to tell her. And although she and "Uncle Emil" would have done anything for me, they seemed to understand that I couldn't let myself accept too much from them. If I got too close, I knew, I might reveal the terrible drama going on at home.

But there was one thing Paula and Emil offered that I couldn't refuse: access to a zoo. As it happened, Emil was the general director of the Sparkassen in Bremen, the German equivalent of an American building and loan society. After World War II this kind of bank was a powerful force in rebuilding Germany's cities. So Emil was on the board of directors of just about everything of significance in Bremen; luckily for me, he was the sponsor and founder of the Bremen Zoo.

My aunt and uncle knew of my love for animals and, as a present, arranged for me to have access to the zoo and its library at all times. From the time I was about ten, I went there every chance I had. Weekends, school holidays—I was always there. At first I didn't do much. I just hung around and observed the animals. As I became friendlier with the people who worked at the zoo, I asked if I couldn't help take care of the animals. The veterinarian let me go on his rounds with him, and soon I had permission to help the animal handlers clean the cages of tame animals, like the flamingos.

As much as I loved flamingos, my big dream was to enter the habitat of the zoo's

Roy—A bear hug then, a bear hug now

beautiful tigress. But that was impossible. She was so ferocious she was even a problem for the handlers; she lived by herself in an enormous cage. It was her loneliness I responded to; because she was so dangerous that no one could relate to her, she didn't have much contact with people.

20

Not far from the tigress was something a little smaller, a cheetah named Chico. This was to be my first love affair with an exotic animal and, eventually, the link between Siegfried, magic, and me. Chico had been caught in the wilds of Somalia and was, at two years old, still not tamed. If I was going to enter his cage, I had to establish a relationship through the fence.

It so happens that a cheetah can be made to purrrrr like a house cat—if you can just get on its wavelength. As I had befriended many stray cats, I was able to sense Chico's emotions a lot more easily than I might have a tiger's. And so I began. I spent months talking to Chico through the iron bars, slowly building up his trust. Every day before I reached the zoo, I gave a special whistle call. By the time I appeared at the fence, Chico had returned my whistle with a chirping birdlike sound that was so sensitive you would never associate it with a powerful animal.

The animal handlers sensed what was going on and gave me permission to enter Chico's den. I learned to take care of him: I scrubbed out his quarters; I brushed his coat; I fed him. Eventually he allowed me to put a collar and leash on him and take him out for walks. It didn't take Chico long to be spoiled by my attentions, and he became a one-person animal. That made him a problem: If I wasn't there, the groomers couldn't enter his habitat. So I ended up going to the zoo every day to take care of him.

I spent so much time with Chico that the zoo became like my home. Chico and Hexe were my family, my closest confidants. In the quiet of the cheetah's den I would tell him little stories and speak from my soul to his.

Siegfried

When I turned fourteen, it was time for me to leave school and learn a profession. I went to work in a carpet factory and studied carpet weaving. It was soon clear that my talent lay in the more aesthetic area of designing, so I started to design carpets. But I knew that carpet designing was not my destiny; my passion was still show business.

I never stopped performing my magic and comedy on the weekends, and my aspirations were beginning to outgrow my hometown. I couldn't talk about this with anyone, even Father Johann; for him, magic could never be more than an amusing hobby. As a career, though, magic was blasphemy. The laws of Catholicism didn't tolerate it.

Nor could I confide in my family. To my mother, "entertainer" or "magician" was no different from "Gypsy." And Gypsies evoked a world of traveling circuses and street performers—and the kind of hand-to-mouth life no mother envisions for her son.

There was another reason I couldn't talk to anyone. I wasn't exactly sure what kind of entertainer I wanted to be. All I was certain of was that I'd never figure anything out if I stayed in my hometown. It was too claustrophobic, its inhabitants too narrow-minded. There was no room for growth—personal or professional. And as I grew older, I realized I was totally misunderstood by my family and friends.

On weekends I would climb to the highest point of the Bavarian Alps and look out over this majestic vista and dream about my future. Or I would go to the little theater in my village. I knew where the key was hidden, and at night I would let myself in, turn the spotlight on, open the velvet curtain, and stand at the foot of the stage. I would hear the music, see my audience, listen for the applause, and my fantasy would temporar-

Siegfried leaving home in search of his magic mountain

ily be realized. Quite simply I wanted a new identity. I wasn't happy with the way I was perceived; I didn't want to go through life as my father's son. When I performed in a theater, I was the happiest person alive: I was someone different. I wanted to be different in life as well.

At seventeen I earned my diploma in carpet designing and decided to leave home. I had no idea where I would go or what I would do. My ambition was a simple one: to be some place where I had contact with lots of people. There was, however, one obstacle to my ambition: I didn't know how to tell my mother.

Ours was a complicated relationship. Because she was unable to express affection, I was never able to show my love. Yet I knew she loved me. If I weren't sure of that, I wouldn't have had any trouble telling her I was leaving home.

True to her ways, when I told my mother I was going away, all she said was: "If you leave now, you never have to come back again." This sounds like a terrible thing to tell your child, but I knew that her words didn't match her heart. She was truly hurt by my decision. She couldn't understand it. By this time my older brother, Marinus, had taken over the family business. My sister, Margot, who had wanted to be a nun since she was eight, had gone off to the convent. My father offered little, if any, companionship. My mother was essentially by herself. My decision to leave made her feel, in her own eyes, like a failure as a mother. Her stinging remark to me was her last-ditch effort to make me stay.

R*oy*

At thirteen a German boy had two choices. Either you left school and entered a vocational college to learn a trade, or you took the exam to continue with your secondary education. One thing I knew: I wanted neither of these options, particularly more formal schooling.

My mother, of course, was desperate for me to stay in school. Baffled by my resistance, she went to the director of the school to see if he could shed some light on the problem. He didn't understand either. He said I had great capabilities, but my refusal to do the work was in the way. And then he asked my mother if there was anything he should know. With great difficulty, she told him—breaking down as she finally let it all out—the story of our homelife.

The director was shattered. He told her that she couldn't permit it anymore, that she couldn't let her boy go one more day living under those conditions. He then had a private meeting with me and alluded to the fact that he knew there was a problem and that he wanted to help. But dynamite wouldn't have made me tell him, and to get him off the trail, I assured him that everything was fine at home.

And so the time came—with many intermezzi in between—when I had to leave school and, in my view, the town as well. I didn't want to leave my mother alone with my stepfather or have her disappointed in me, but I had to get out of there. Somewhere else the world was wholesome; it was time I found that place.

Siegfried

The magic mountain for this German teenager in 1956 was a small resort hotel in Lago di Garda, Italy. I started out as a dishwasher. Then I began to serve. In a few months I was working behind the bar.

Siegfried at Lago di Garda, 1956

The hotel opened up a new world for me. For the first time I felt appreciated. People liked me and said I had a good personality. So I decided to learn the hotel business, to stay in Italy for three years and earn another diploma.

I learned more than just the hotel business. I saw the way other people lived, the way families responded to one another. I would watch with a certain envy how the families staying in the hotel kissed and hugged one another and how nicely the parents treated their children. I hadn't known that existed. And so I decided that when I returned home for a visit, I was going to hug my mother.

I planned it all in my head. I would arrive at the house and ring the bell, my mother would come to the door, and I would throw my arms around her and give her a huge hug. I was anxious about this moment for months. As the date of my trip home grew closer, the anticipation made me too nervous to sleep.

The day finally arrived. Everything went as I had planned—until my mother opened the door. Before I could reach out to embrace her, she beat me to the punch and said, "You're back," as if I had just gone around the corner for a few minutes. But I wasn't fooled; I knew there was something else going on inside her. I felt very bad for her and for me that neither of us could get beyond ourselves to show our love.

Aside from my emotional growth, there was a great deal going on with my magic. At the hotel I noticed that after a few nights the guests were bored, so to liven it up, I began to do magic. In the evening I did little tricks at the bar while I tended the drinks. I also trotted out my Bavarian comedy routine, but it didn't work; these people were too sophisticated.

Thank God for that realization. For what I learned is that the surest way to universal applause is through magic. Rich, poor, middle-class, educated, uneducated—magic cuts across all the barriers. It can be understood by everyone, and in some way or another it attracts everyone.

After I had completed my three years at Lago di Garda, I got a position at a resort in Brig, Switzerland. The owners of the hotel took an instant liking to me and began to treat me like a part of their family. At that time it was very unusual for a blond, blue-eyed German named Siegfried to be treated so well by the Swiss as they weren't too excited by us Germans after the war.

The hotel's owners wanted to groom me to run the place, but once again magic was too strong. I performed at parties that were held there. Soon I felt ready for the next challenge. Another hotel didn't intrigue me. A ship did.

I sent away for the brochures of ocean liners and was immediately swept off my feet. The photos showed a dance floor, an orchestra; it looked very glamorous. It also looked like the perfect opportunity to develop my magic into more than just a hobby.

I hired on as a steward on the TS *Bremen*, a beautiful German luxury liner that sailed from the port of Bremerhaven to New York and back. I began in tourist class; by the return trip I had already worked my way up to first class.

In the evenings the crew went downstairs to the bar. My first oceanic audience, I thought, and I began to perform my magic for them, making sure that one day the news eventually reached the captain's ears. Just as I hoped, the captain summoned me.

"I hear you do magic," he said. "Show me some."

I quickly returned with my bag of tricks and went into my act. "That's enough," he said when I had done only a few tricks. "Tonight you perform for the passengers."

My plan had worked.

That night I did sleight of hand tricks with cards, coins, and cigarettes. And for old times' sake, I swallowed twenty razor blades. By this time I had perfected it. I swallowed them, followed by a long string, and then magically made the blades reappear hooked on to the string. I was so well received that on the next crossing the captain got rid of the passenger talent show—the only form of live entertainment that existed on the ship—and had me do a half hour of magic as the entertainment.

I didn't have to imagine my audience anymore. I had them—live—and I was in heaven. I had found a niche for myself that was really about

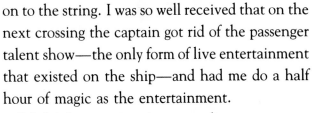

The ship that sailed us into freedom and set the stage for our life's voyage

being a performer. No longer did I feel that I was wasting my time with a hobby that would never take me anywhere. Now I was pursuing the career of my dreams. I even gave myself a stage name. I was Delmare* the Magician. My only obstacle now was to overcome my constant seasickness!

I had always believed I was destined for something wonderful and interesting. But my intuition wasn't strong enough to tell me that a little magic act on a ship would be the turning point; for me, from the moment I went to Italy, every small good thing that happened to me was the turning point! Now the joy of performing in front of an audience was my definition of success.

*Delmare means "from the sea" in Spanish.

That's why, when people ask me, "Well, Siegfried, when do you think you made it in your life?"

I always have the same answer: "I thought I made it the day I left home."

oy

Where do you go at thirteen, an age when most kids today still need baby-sitters? The answer was logical for me, who lived right by the ocean. It was a ship belonging to the North German Lloyd.

I hired on without my family's permission. When the time came to sail, I had the decency to tell them, but I didn't give them an option. My mother was shattered. And my stepfather, though he didn't like to show it, had always had high hopes for me as well. I was unshakable. I told them that if they didn't give me their blessing, I would just go and then they would worry where I was.

To make my mother feel better, I told her that I wanted to go out and see the world and that I was in fact learning a profession, the hotel business. This wasn't really a lie. Through my work on the ship, I did end up getting my diploma, and when I was seventeen, I opened my very own bed and breakfast in Blexen, another village across the Weser River from Bremerhaven.

All my determination looked a little silly when I arrived at the dock for my first Atlantic crossing. I was still a runt, so scrawny I looked no more than the age of ten. I didn't even have enough money to buy a ship's jacket—not that I could have found one to fit. Nevertheless, I proudly reported to the boat and walked up that gangplank as if I were the captain.

The excitement of my first voyage and the enthusiasm of my newfound freedom were temporarily blurred as I watched the crowds at the dock waving good-bye to their loved ones. When your ship is going out to sea and the orchestra is playing "Muss Ich denn" and "Auf Wiedersehen" and there's no one waving you off, well, that makes an impact. All the hurts, the loneliness, the emotional dramas of my childhood are, for me, bottled up in this one scene.

If I thought my spirit couldn't be broken any more than it already was, I was severely mistaken. Nothing had prepared me for the experience of seasickness. For the first and last time ever I was a hopeless pessimist and seriously considered jumping overboard.

Little trouper that I was, I hid my misery enough to charm the captain of the ship. I started off as a bellboy in first class, but the captain took an immediate liking to me— he probably knew I was too ill to be on deck in the rough Atlantic—and soon appointed me his personal bellboy.

As a result of my prestigious promotion, I didn't have to worry about not having my own ship's jacket. I was given a wonderful pint-size uniform with a thousand stars and stripes and a smart little cap. Now I looked like a storybook image of an ocean liner bellboy—tiny as a thimble, expressive brown eyes, so vulnerable the wind could blow me over.

Image didn't count for much when the ship almost sank. On the fifth day of our eight-day crossing, I brought the captain his evening cocktail, only to be told to go below deck right away, we were coming into some rough seas. I proceeded to make my way down. Right underneath the next deck there were enormous windows. I looked out and saw that the waves were indeed house-high. It was like being in a valley with peaks and tolls. Suddenly I spotted a sailor in his uniform floating right by me; apparently he had gone on deck to tighten things up and the waves had taken him. And he wasn't the only crew member washed overboard; before the sea calmed down, many more sailors were lost.

Roy, the bellboy, smiling at the world—crisp, clean, and cheerful—charming captains and passengers

The passengers were in a complete panic. With two other bellboys, I had to control the stampede of passengers as they tried to get to the lifeboats. The ship was in danger of sinking, but they were making it worse: More weight on that side might have caused us to capsize. Talk about a performance! I had to stand there with a jolly smile on my face and reassure the passengers that we were merely passing through a patch of rough sea and that the thing to do was to obey the captain's order to follow us down to the dining room for lunch.

At this point I went into the pantry and helped serve this improbable meal. The pantry was flooded, and not only did I have to roll up my

29

pants legs so they wouldn't get wet, but I had to do something about my prize possession, my one pair of patent leather shoes. In a flash I had them off and safely stashed on top of the refrigerator, where the salt water couldn't hurt them. Such were my priorities.

At three-thirty the next morning the *United States*, the fastest ship on the Atlantic, came to our rescue. Because our motors were damaged, it towed us into New York Harbor. By that time our SOS signals had been transmitted through the radio and alerted the German media of our troubles.

We had to spend a week in New York waiting for the boat to be repaired. I knew my parents were probably sick with fear that I had been lost at sea, so I sent them a telegram.

The excitement of being in New York City was too much, and I decided to do some investigating. Without a map, speaking no English, I left Pier 88 at Forty-eighth Street and proceeded to walk north. I walked for miles, totally mesmerized by the enormous buildings, the craziness of the traffic, and the contrasts of the people on the street. I finally stopped to look up at a street sign and realized I had walked about a hundred blocks. By now I was exhausted and lost. I noticed a parked bus across the street. It was emply except for the driver, who was a huge, old black man. I banged on the door and in German explained that I needed to go back to the boat. Of course, he had no idea. I remembered that the English word for *Wasser* was "water," so in my poor pronunciation I said over and over again, "vota, vota." (Even today, I don't say it much better.) The driver was no less confused, so I took out a pad and pencil and drew a boat with some water, pounded my chest, and pointed south. He motioned for me to come inside the bus, and with me as the only passenger, he drove me back to the pier.

This man's kindness made a lasting impression. When I finally moved to America and often heard people complain about the rude and thoughtless New Yorkers, I always defended them on the basis of my encounter. Thirty years later, when my white tigers were stolen, New York was a much different place from when I was a boy, but I got exactly the same kind of treatment. And when we played at Radio City Music Hall in 1989 and the toughest audience in the world embraced us, I smiled and remembered my man on the bus. This "callous" city has never let me down.

When I returned to Bremerhaven ten days later, a dockside band was there to play the German national anthem. My entire family was there, too. I'm sure they thought that after this experience I had had a big enough taste of the world and would come running down the gangplank, throw my arms around them, and cry, "I'm so glad to be back home." Well, they were wrong. I was a tough little hombre with a will of iron, and there was no question in my mind that I wanted to stay on the ship.

There was only one problem, one very big problem: I didn't have Chico with me. And the homesickness I felt for him would have been my only reason to abandon ship. After I had made my decision to leave home, my Aunt Paula, who thought she might lose me forever if I went, gave Chico to me—outright—thinking, of course, that would make me stay. When her plan failed, she said I could take Chico out of the zoo to live with me, but only if I stayed in Bremen.

There were times I almost gave in. After each crossing the first thing I did when I got off the boat was go see Chico. Long before I entered the gates of the zoo, I would give my call and he would be waiting at the fence for me as if I had never left. I would go inside his den—by now covered with the postcards I sent him while on my travels—and lie down with him on my lap. And then he would nuzzle his sweet head on mine and purr like a sewing machine for hours. It was like a vacation for both of us.

Then the day would come when I had to leave again. Chico always knew. His big, sad brown eyes and melancholy calling sounds followed me all the way out of the zoo and haunted me until my next return. But no matter what heartache I felt when I left Chico, no matter how much pressure my aunt put on me, I knew that my decision to leave home was the right one.

Slowly my soul was beginning to heal. There really was a bright, better world out there, and I couldn't turn away from it now. And I knew something would eventually happen that would make it possible for Chico to be with me.

Free as the wind
Roy roaming the fields with Chico

ACT TWO

Everything you can imagine is real,

—PABLO PICASSO

SEVENTH ANNUAL
LAS VEGAS ENTERTAINMENT AWARDS

ACADEMY OF VARIETY AND CABARET ARTISTS

Best of Las Vegas Award

Jimmy

THE "JIMMY" DURANTE
BEST OF LAS VEGAS AWARD
Siegfried & Roy
SPECIALTY ACT OF THE YEAR
1976

ENTERTAINMENT PERSONALITIES OF THE
Presented to
SIEGFRIED & ROY

THE INTERNATIONAL MAGIC AWARDS

HOUDINI AWARD

5th Annual Las Vegas
Entertainment Awards
1975
PRODUCTION ACT OF THE YEAR
Hallelujah Hollywood
Siegfried & Roy

34

Siegfried

My show soon became so popular that all the people who wanted to see me perform couldn't be accommodated in one show. The solution was for me to do two shows—one for first class, another for tourist. To sustain a half hour act, I had to come up with more material. And so, in the great tradition of magic, I introduced rabbits and doves into my act.

Now I had animals. Props. Light cues. It was too much for one person to cover and still perform. But as I had no assistant, I asked a steward—anyone would do—to help me with the show.

One evening I was late setting up. As I hurried upstairs, I bumped into the young boy whose cabin was right across the hall from mine. I had never said as much as hello to Roy. Rather than take the time to search for one of the stewards I knew, I asked him if he would assist me that night.

I don't remember how the show went, but afterward, as was my custom, I offered to buy my assistant of the evening a beer. Roy was like no one I'd worked with. Instead of complimenting me or asking the standard questions, he sat silently drinking his beer. The minutes dragged on. I realized I wasn't going to get anything out of him unless I asked.

"Well, what did you think of the show?"

No answer.

I repeated the question.

Still no comment.

I did, however, see a flicker of response as he started to fidget. He was clearly uncomfortable. But at least he was reacting.

Finally Roy spoke. "Well, the audience really liked you. And it's great that you can do all those tricks," he said. "But quite honestly I didn't really like the show that much. The magic seems so predictable."

No one had ever said that to me. I could feel the anger rising up. But I quickly rationalized it. This boy—this infant—was just too young to understand my talents. Clearly he was a smug little punk who didn't know any better.

R*oy*

I liked the show more than I said. Dancing canes floating around his body, shimmering gold pieces appearing and disappearing, a scarlet red silk scarf that produced birds out of thin air, what wasn't to like? As a matter of fact, I was in awe. But I couldn't tell him that, for I had a plan.

Once Siegfried got past his anger, he asked me a constructive question: If I were so smart, what would I do to improve his act?

As it happened, I had an answer.

First show at sea

**Roy—from bellboy to steward with no idea of the
uncharted waters soon to be encountered**

Perhaps not to his problem, but certainly to mine. For a while now the family pressure
to return home had been increasing. Hanging over my head was the possibility that if I
didn't return, they would get rid of Chico. But if I could get him on the boat, my family
would no longer have a hold on me. When I saw Siegfried performing with his rabbit
and doves, I immediately thought that if he could have his animals on board, then why
couldn't I have my cheetah with me?

"If you can make a rabbit and doves appear and disappear," I asked, "could you do the
same thing with a cheetah?"

Siegfried stared at me. He didn't have a response. I repeated my question. I could tell
that I had really put him on the spot. For perhaps a minute neither of us spoke.

"In magic," he said at last, "anything is possible."

Siegfried

"In magic anything is possible."

Of course, I said that. I wasn't about to let this wise guy think otherwise. Who knew he had a pet cheetah? Or that he'd be so bold as to suggest that I incorporate *his* animal into *my* show!

I didn't take him seriously. I was sure he'd had a few beers too many or just liked to fantasize. A cheetah! For me that animal existed only in the wilds of Africa or locked away in a zoo. Who in the world—except for Josephine Baker—could possibly have a cheetah for a *pet*?

I didn't see Roy for the rest of the trip. We completed the crossing and returned to Bremerhaven. Frankly, I forgot about him.

On our next voyage we had been out at sea for a few days when Roy knocked on my cabin door. Before I could say anything, he raised his fingers to his mouth and said with a hush under his breath he had a secret suprise for me. Curiously I went across the hall and looked into his cabin—and there was this beast. I froze in fear.

 **R**oy

I wish I had a photograph of Siegfried's face the first time he saw Chico crouched on my bunk bed. There they were, eyeball to eyeball—only one showing his teeth. Chico was tame with me, but he was still essentially a wild, exotic animal, and he reacted like one to this stranger. Siegfried took a gigantic leap backward from my spotted, snarling, spitting bundle, which was, in all reality, fully prepared to attack.

I suppose I could have convinced Siegfried that the cheetah was real some other way. But I'd been festering ever since we'd had our conversation at the bar. I knew he didn't believe a thing I said. He thought I was wet behind the ears—a kid with an overactive imagination.

Well, he was right about that. I was determined to show him I could do some magic, too. At Bremen I had liberated Chico from the zoo, smuggled him on board in my laundry bag, and kept him hidden in my cabin until we were too far at sea for the captain to turn back if he found out.

Siegfried

After I got over being scared to death, I considered what it meant to have a wild animal on board. And I knew we were in big trouble.

For his part Roy was quite enthusiastic about the whole thing. "Well, what do you think?" he kept asking.

"It's amazing," I finally said, not knowing what to think or do. "You really were serious."

And then I got serious. I told him how wrong it was for him to do this. He could lose his job and mine. When the captain found out, I said, he would surely throw us off the ship.

Roy was completely cool. "Don't tell him. Wait until you do your magic with the cheetah, and then he'll understand. He'll like it. I promise you."

The cheetah in my magic? Boy, this kid had some grand illusions. I hadn't begun to consider it, and let me tell you, the cheetah was a bigger problem than the captain. Could I do something with a large animal and one that was untame? The show was in three days. Could I do it on such short notice? I explained to Roy that developing an illusion required preparation and rehearsal time. You don't just snap your fingers, and *voilà*! But from a theatrical point of view, I had to admit, Roy's challenge was exciting, for the cheetah would certainly give the ultimate element of surprise in the show. Perhaps in that setting the captain might even feel well disposed toward the beast.

I went to the ship's carpenter, and we built a box. I then remembered seeing a stuffed leopard in the souvenir shop. A close enough resemblance. I bought it, cut the head, tail, and legs off, then sewed each part up individually so the stuffing wouldn't come out. Then I put it back together so it looked new.

On the evening of the performance I did all my usual magic. Then Roy brought up the box. By this time the captain, the stewards, and the rest of the crew realized I was going to introduce something new. Roy went offstage, returning with a basket that contained the stuffed leopard. I began to tear it apart limb by limb, throwing each piece high up in the air and into the box. And then, as if the trick were done, I closed the lid.

The ship's band reached a crescendo; the drummer gave a timpani roll; the spotlight tightened. And then slowly, with impeccably good dramatic timing, the lid opened—and the cheetah jumped out, mercifully secured by a chain. This was, however, a new circumstance for Chico. He was completely shaken by all the commotion: people, applause, and music. He looked straight out into the disbelieving audience. Hissing and snarling, he jumped off the box. He was as scared as they were and had to protect himself. With one eye on Roy, his only security and the other eye on the audience, he walked to the end of the dance floor.

The only sound that was made during his exit was the crack, crack, crack of the chain on the parquet floor. For Roy, who was as stunned as anyone, had let go of the chain. Instead of leading him out, he had to follow beside the cheetah. Slowly and dramatically they climbed the grand staircase, and when Chico reached the top, like a prima donna, he turned around and regally faced his audience.

It was my first and *our* first standing ovation.

To see something like that in the middle of the Atlantic . . . well, it was quite sophisticated for the time. The audience went wild with excitement.

The captain did not.

Roy

Sure enough, Captain Rossinger called both of us to his stateroom after the show. With ice in his voice, he told us that if Mr. Nagle, the American president of the North German Lloyd, hadn't been on board with his wife, he would have stopped the show. There was no question about it: Once we arrived in New York, the cheetah would have to be flown back to Germany. Our employment would be terminated upon our arrival at Bremerhaven. And all that was final.

I didn't feel bad for me because I didn't have that much to lose. But I felt terrible for subjecting Siegfried to my plan and ruining his career on the ship. I tried to conjure up different plans that might reverse the captain's decision, but not even in my imagination could I think of anything that might work.

The next day I was walking down the hallway of the first-class compartments, and a very attractive, clearly sophisticated, and totally American couple stopped to introduce themselves. They were none other than Mr. and Mrs. Nagle. They loved the show, they said; they called it the best entertainment they had ever seen on a ship. Such an act deserved a bigger audience, Mr. Nagle said. He proposed to give us one—on the firm's Caribbean cruise liners. With a hearty American pat on the back, he congratulated me, told me that Siegfried and I had a big career ahead of us, and invited us to visit him at his New York office.

Soulmates
Roy and Chico

In return, I gave him a blank stare.

Seeing that I looked perplexed, Mr. Nagle asked if anything was wrong. I told him his compliments were very flattering, but unfortunately we had been fired. This made no impression on him whatsoever. "Don't worry about it, my boy," said Mr. Nagle, "I'll have a word with the captain."

Now we were in great shape.

Mr. Nagle was as good as his word. One thing he couldn't do, though, was change the captain's opinion of us; from then on, the captain was our enemy. The night after we performed with the cheetah, we were scheduled to serve in the dining room, and when Siegfried and I entered, the passengers applauded. The captain happened to be following right behind us, but when he made his entrance, all he got was a polite nod. He considered himself the king of the ship and its only celebrity. The attention that the passengers continued to lavish on Siegfried and me—and Chico—never ceased to irritate him.

I don't know what bothered him more, the attention or the money we made from the cheetah. He thought the excitement we had generated would quickly die down. He had no idea that our imaginations could propel us to create a second business opportunity for ourselves on *his* ship.

But we had sensed that Chico was such a sensation the passengers might like souvenir photographs of themselves with him. So we put a table on the promenade deck, set two palm trees behind it, and made an agreement with the boat photographer. It cost $1.50 to have your photo taken with the captain; because we thought it was infinitely more special to have one with a cheetah, we charged $2.50.

At the end of the cruise the captain discovered what we had done. And he was furious. He learned that almost all of the eight hundred passengers had their photos taken. By doing a quick calculation in his head, he figured out that between our salary and what we were making on the photographs, we were earning almost as much as he did.

Considering what the company was paying us for our performance, we certainly felt entitled to that bit of extra money. Because we were being paid as stewards, they didn't think they needed to pay us for our performances, so our only reward was the bottle of Blue Nun white wine that we split after each show. Not that we were mercenary about any of it; we were so excited and lucky still to be on the ship, we didn't really care.

As our popularity grew, our "pay" was increased to a bottle of wine each. We weren't that fond of wine, so the next time we arrived in New York, we went to see Mr. Nagle and asked if we might be paid. He agreed to give us twenty-five marks—a bit less than ten dollars. We considered that quite a coup. I'll never forget the first time we arrived at Bremerhaven with those twenty-five marks extra in our pockets. Siegfried and I bicycled to my hometown. We were so jolly, riding through the little streets next to each other, all the while slapping each other on the back because we thought we'd really made it in show business. The next thing we knew, a policeman was motioning for us to stop.

Because we were riding side by side on this tiny dirt road—which was barely wide enough for his police car—he gave us a fine oif twenty-five marks. And so there went our first salary.

Siegfried

We became the talk of the ship. As a result of our success and the excitement our show seemed to create, the passengers were drinking more, and we in turn became quite a money-maker for the ship. This pleased the management so much that we were relieved of our duties as stewards and not only were allowed to perform but also were put in charge of all boat entertainment, which meant hiring other live acts to perform on our nights off. Before Roy and me, there had never been live entertainment on German cruise lines; their idea of recreation had been bingo, dancing, and movies. With the formation of our act we paved the way for a new standard of oceanic entertainment.

And just as Mr. Nagle said, we were put on the Caribbean cruises.

All this was great, except that now that we were performing more, the same people were watching the show, and that meant we had to keep it fresh and add new things.

Eins, zwei, suffa!
Celebrating Oktoberfest with my Aunt Paula after Siegfried and I were put in charge of all ship entertainment

Our two favorite girls
Aunt Paula and my mother, Johanna, celebrating New Year's Eve on the ship with their two favorite boys

Because of those expectations, I reached a new level in my magic. I started trying new things all the time to keep it successful.

When I wasn't working, I was alone in my little cabin. For three years I lived like a monk, spending my spare time perfecting my act and thinking up new ideas for it. It was the most fantastic schooling I could have had. I got theories from my books, but that was all. The bulk of my learning was through performing.

People sometimes think magic is hard to grasp intellectually. Actually its principles are simple. What is difficult is coordinating the elements—how you handle the situation you're in, how to read your audience and understand the way they think so you can manipulate effectively.

On the ship not only was I forced to build a repertoire, but because I didn't have the luxury of a stage and I worked surrounded by people on all sides, it was difficult to achieve certain illusions. So I had to stretch way beyond the limits of my imagination. The experience taught me to create wonderment and fantasy out of the barest of essentials.

R_{oy}

Siegfried realized very quickly that Chico had one master: *me!* In order to keep the cheetah in the show, we had to become partners. Without even realizing it, I had gone into show business, which I had never had any intention of doing. Truthfully I hadn't done any long-range planning once I smuggled Chico on board and got Siegfried to use him in the show. Even when Siegfried brought me into his act, my focus wasn't on becoming a magician.

No, my focus was all on Siegfried and what he had to offer.

Siegfried was, very simply, the key to a different world. He had the power to put my cheetah in the show. He also had the power to bring me into a wholesome world, for in illusions, there's a beginning, a middle, and a happy or, at the very least, an interesting ending. I believed in that sequence, but I'd just never experienced it; little did I know what it took to create that happy finish! So yes, there was admiration, but there was also selfishness: His was the world I wanted to escape to, live in, and enjoy. It was an extension of the make-believe world I'd lived in for so long.

Actually it took only a sentence. When Siegfried said, "In magic anything is possible," those became the most important words in my life—and they still are. Think of it: For

Lightweight saves heavyweight

A smile returns to Roy's face after saving Chico from an attempted leap overboard.
The attention we got as a result of our show enraged the captain, and he had blown the ship's
siren and foghorn with Chico standing close by in hope that it would frighten him and he would
take a flying dive into the Atlantic. This cruel incident was just part of the captain's master
plot to destroy our career.

a sixteen-year-old kid who had spent most of his life dipping in and out of his dreams and fantasies because the real world was too harsh for him, to hear someone endorse all those dreams was magic itself.

45

That's why I say that I felt secure from the moment I met Siegfried—more secure than I had ever felt with any two-legged creature. As I never had a very close relationship with my brothers, I suppose subconsciously Siegfried became the brother I never had. But beyond the fraternal feeling, I believed in him, perhaps more than he did himself.

Siegfried appreciated my confidence in him, and he repaid it by teaching me everything I needed to know in order to become a real part of the act. He taught me the logic behind the execution of the manipulations. He showed me how a magician has to build the sequences properly in order to arrive at the desired climax, how he has to think the opposite from his spectators, and, most important of all, that a good magician manipulates the minds of the audience.

He would test a new effect on me, and if I could figure it out, then he knew he needed to polish it or change his emphasis. We still do this today with our illusions.

What did I teach Siegfried?

Well, naturally about animals. But it wasn't what I taught him; it was what I showed him. And that was optimism. Enthusiasm. Fantasy. The desire to break with rules and tradition, which often provoked a clash of personalities. And, of course, unlimited self-confidence. For my ambition was very simple: I wanted Siegfried to become the greatest living magician of our time. And I vowed to help him do it. Siegfried wasn't exactly flattered. He saw my ambition for him as what it was—a weighty responsibility. That was what I intended. I wanted to give him a goal.

Siegfried

When I told Roy that in magic anything was possible, I said it with a certain arrogance. He took it literally. Because of that, he forced me to meet a new challenge in my craft. Roy was, in short, the turning point of my career. And so was his cheetah. It didn't take me long to realize the potential that this wonderful animal held for me. This was more interesting than pulling rabbits out of a hat.

Chico made me different. And that is the true secret of magic.

A magician needs a signature. With the cheetah I had one. Even if people couldn't remember our names, they would surely recall "the two fellows with the cheetah." The cheetah was special.

And so was Roy.

A magician's lie is the truth and the truth is his lie.

Early on I saw that Roy was more of an illusionist than I am. He lives in his dreams. He invents his reality, he sees it in color, he cherishes its beauty—and he's blind to the obstacles.

The obstacles are all I see. Magic starts with a fantasy, but once I have an idea, I know there are a million problems to solve before the illusion works. In ignoring those problems, Roy presented me a challenge bigger than his cheetah: him!

Fortunately I recognized right away how strongly Roy believed in me. And my goal changed: From then on I never wanted him to be disappointed in me. I had to rise above myself in order to let him think I was secure.

Roy

After all these years Siegfried is still the person I respect and admire the most, and in a way, he's the only hero I've ever had. I don't tell him that very often. Because the fact is we are a bit like the elements—opposite ones—and have been since day one. We don't actually disagree with each other, but our perception of whatever we're working on or should be doing is, most of the time, very different.

That's the way our relationship has always worked. It's also why our partnership keeps on working. Siegfried comes up with an idea for an illusion, and I take it to some faraway, unattainable place. He likes to say that he is too little, I am too much. I begin to fantasize and run away with his idea. He then levels me to reality. Somehow we meet in the middle, and at last we create something together.

Sometimes it works the other way. I'll have an idea that is too wild and could never be materialized, but something about it will set off a spark in Siegfried that forces him to go in a different direction. Then I have to go the other way to get what I want.

Siegfried

Thank God I get bored easily.

Another magician might have relied too much on Chico and run his act into the ground with him. I soon tired of doing the cheetah illusion the way we originally conceived it. My objection was that we weren't really creating an illusion with Chico. It was a surprise moment, nothing more. I wanted to make him more of an embellishment.

And that meant using Roy more.

In the beginning Roy didn't really take part in the theatrics. He handled the cheetah. He was in charge of the rabbit. His first integration into the show was when I levitated him, an illusion that I had never attempted before and one that proved difficult in such a small setting. Roy, however, levitated himself flawlessly, even though the ship was rocking from side to side.

I realized that if I wanted to achieve more with the cheetah, I had to incorporate Roy into the illusion. So with the ship carpenters building me things from sketches, not even knowing what they were actually creating, and Roy and me working down in our little cabins, we developed our first trunk illusion: an adaptation of Houdini's famous metamorphosis.

Roy got himself handcuffed, tied in a sack, and locked inside the trunk. Now came the classic trunk exchange. I jumped on top of the sealed trunk, slipped a cloth hoop over me, and, in a split second, the cloth dropped and Roy appeared in my place on top of the trunk. He then opened it and I was inside in the sack and handcuffed. As a finale we did our original illusion, and we both tossed the stuffed animal pieces in the trunk, and the cheetah popped out.

When we did the metamorphosis for the first time, Roy thought it would be more impressive if we did costume changes inside the trunk, but with an amusing nautical twist. So Roy started the illusion wearing a bellboy's uniform, but when he escaped from the trunk, he was dressed as an American sailor. I started the illusion wearing my tuxedo and cape, but after the transformation I appeared in a captain's uniform. And there was a little joke about that uniform; instead of the standard four stripes on the sleeves, mine had five. That, of course, antagonized our dear captain, as, I suppose, we intended it to.

The metamorphosis satisfied me for a time, but I wanted to develop a third exchange—with Chico. In our new version, after our trunk exchange, instead of throwing stuffed pieces into the basket, Roy jumped inside the trunk, I closed it, and with a dramatic drumroll I opened it and Roy had transformed into the cheetah.

It was this illusion that really started the organic growth of our act. All illusions are derived from five basic ideas: appearance, disappearance, transformation, levitation, and sawing. The challenge for a magician is to put these principles into his own wrapping or adapt them to his given situation. Because I had to make it work for our situation—Roy's, Chico's, and mine—it was natural that the metamorphosis would evolve into a triple effect.

And out of that came our trademark of effortlessly rolling three illusions into one.

R*oy*

And out of that came our destiny.

ACT THREE

It is not enough to conquer; one must know how to seduce.

—VOLTAIRE

Roy

As time went on, Siegfried and I realized that we had stretched our imagination to the limits of what we could create on the ship. We were fortunate to have met passengers who were involved in show business and offered us contacts. As we had become comfortable with our success on the boat, the first of these opportunities was a harsh but realistic introduction to the big world of show biz.

Elmarie Wendel, a successful German-American comedienne who also performed on the ship, was one of our biggest fans. She had been telling us for ages that she thought we were wasting our talent on the ship and that America was the perfect place for us. With each crossing, she kept pushing us to see Mark Leddy, her agent in New York. Apparently he was the best and brightest agent for live acts, he had the best connections in television—like *The Ed Sullivan Show*—and he booked his clients in theaters all over America—even Las Vegas.

About the time we were considering leaving the boat, we arrived in New York and decided to follow Elmarie's advice. With a letter of introduction in hand, we arrived at the office of Mr. Mark Leddy. We had heard for three years that we were brilliant and had begun to believe it. We strode into Mr. Leddy's office with enough confidence to launch a thousand airplanes. We just knew he was gonna love us.

Siegfried

He might have loved us if we hadn't been German, but Mr. Leddy was of German Jewish extraction, and

54

The beginning of our ever-changing metamorphosis. Twenty-eight years later, it still captivates our audience—only the trunk remains unchanged.

although we thought World War II was long over, the sight of a blond, blue-eyed young fellow—the embodiment of Hitler's "Aryan" race—introducing himself in a thick German accent as Siegfried was enough to stop this agent cold.

We explained our signature trunk illusion with Chico and our other illusions. We finished, eager to hear what Mr. Leddy thought. Instead, he told us how his family had suffered in Germany during World War II. I didn't know what to say. I just stood there taking it in, not quite sure what I was hearing.

It may sound odd to you, but this was the first time I had ever heard anyone talk about the Nazi atrocities. During the war I was too small to know; after the war the subject was suppressed in school, in our homes, indeed in all Germany. The main concern of our people was to forget. So hearing Mr. Leddy rant about the Germans shocked Roy and me to the bone.

Then he got to the subject of our magic. He wasn't impressed. He made it sound as if everything we were doing were really quite ordinary.

At the time my English was not very good, and my comprehension was almost nonexistent. So it took me awhile to understand that no matter what we would have done for him, it was never going to be good enough.

By now I was steaming with anger that Roy and I were being held responsible not only for our country's actions but for our apparent lack of talent. When he finished, I looked him straight in the eye and said in the few words of English that I knew, "Mr. Leddy, I think you vant to tell me that ve are not good enough for you. Vell, I vill tell *you* something. I'm gonna leave here now. And you gonna hear from us."

Roy and I turned on our heels and marched out.

R*oy*

That's Siegfried—great with closing lines.

We slammed the door. Siegfried put his arm around me. "Roy, that was the first time we ever faced an agent, and it's going to be our last. We have to be so good they come to us."

It was a promise we kept; we've never had an agent. In fact, we've never even had a business card. That isn't to say we've gotten over our encounter with Mr. Leddy. Every night at the Mirage we put him in our act—and give him all the credit he's due.

Mr. Leddy's rejection only made us more determined, and we set out to pursue the offer that lay waiting for us in Germany. Frau Fritz, the owner of the Astoria Theater in Bremen, had been a passenger on the ship, and she told us that whenever we had the time, she would book us into her theater for a month-long engagement. Although this wasn't the most secure future, in 1964 we decided to leave the ship and take our chances.

The Astoria was one of the last great vaudeville theaters left in Germany. Because it was a cabaret situation, we had to have two different numbers of fifteen minutes each. So we had to come up with a half hour program that could be divided in two. This was quite a task because we basically had to create a beginning, middle, and an end twice and have two different setups. There were all kinds of new obstacles: a live orchestra with written music, a lighting system we had to direct, the first stagehands we'd ever encountered, and, now that I was fully incorporated into the show, no assistant to deal with the illusions and animals. On top of all that, I gave myself four costume changes to glamorize and enhance the sequences.

I can tell you doing something like this for the first time gives you stage fright. And Siegfried had it so badly that he never wanted to go on any stage ever again. But there was no choice; the train had left the station. For our debut I had a costume designer in Bremen design me a velvet outfit and make Siegfried a cape and top hat, which put a severe dent in our budget.

We'd gone to all this trouble. Now what was I going to do? Two hours before curtain time Siegfried was in the dressing room, totally devastated, saying over and over again, "I can't go on." I took the cover for the cheetah's cage, rolled it up, made a big pillow for Siegfried, and assured him his case of preshow jitters was normal. "Rest," I said. "It will clear your mind."

Well, nothing worked.

I was also a nervous wreck. But someone had to do *something*. I couldn't go to Frau Fritz and tell her we couldn't go on because Siegfried didn't feel like it. And it certainly didn't help matters that the stage manager had been telling Siegfried and me during rehearsals that we were committing professional suicide by trying to perform a full-scale magic show in Germany because the old days were gone forever.

I had one last solution. Siegfried, unlike most people when they're under pressure, always eats. So I got the key to the dressing room, made sure he was resting, locked the windows and the door—from the outside, of course—so he couldn't do a disappearing act on me. I charged over to the train station and bought some bratwurst on buns and Coca-Cola. Siegfried ate the whole thing. With perfect timing, Frau Fritz stopped by to say she thought the rehearsal had been great.

The last thing Siegfried would ever do is admit defeat to Frau Fritz. Instantly becoming the entertainer again, he told her how much he was looking forward to the show. And because she thought it would go well, Siegfried didn't feel so bad anymore.

Considering it was a new adventure, the performance went without any big hitches. I handled all the props and costume changes, laid out everything Siegfried needed for the transitional moments, and made sure I was in place at the right time so I could perform all the illusions with him. In other words, I did everything and was the support behind the entire half hour. Whenever Siegfried had nothing to do for thirty seconds and I wasn't visible, he would say, "I'm waiting for my partner, Roy, but I guess he's new in this place."

You can imagine how wonderful that was for me.

This first experience working off the ship very quickly taught me something about my relationship with Siegfried and the structure of our collaboration. I realized very early that I could never allow us both to feel the same thing at the same time because it would stifle us and we both would be vulnerable. So it was difficult, though necessary, for me to swallow Siegfried's remark in order to keep our relationship working and sane.

Siegfried

It was more than just stage fright that night. It was total fear of the entire situation. This was the first time we had performed off the ship as professionals. How would we be perceived? Were we good enough?

Everyone said we were crazy to go on the road with a full-scale illusion show. Illusionists had traditionally performed in vaudeville theaters, and those theaters were closing. There was a new trend, nightclubs. And in nightclubs people sat at tables, surrounding the performer.

These changes created two big obstacles for illusionists. Because they depend on proscenium stages, they found themselves unable to work in this setting. The second problem was that the nightclubs that replaced the vaudeville houses were basically striptease joints.

The first obstacle wasn't really an issue for us. Three years on the ship and working in the round had paid off. The second problem was a bit tougher. People weren't lining up to give nightclub contracts to an act that featured an uncaged, exotic animal a few feet from the audience. And the last thing the club owners were looking for were two male magicians. If they wanted to see a magician at all, it was one who had a generously endowed, scantily dressed female assistant. So our first task was to create a demand for what we were doing.

With the act we had performed on the ship, we decided to try to beat the obstacles. It was fine at the Astoria and Hamburg theaters because of the traditional stage. But after that we were playing in nightclubs, and doing the metamorphosis in that situation was tricky. On the ship we'd had carpenters building props for us; when you were moving from one limited engagement to another, there was no such help. And there were no entrances, no backstages, no place to conceal your equipment, no stagehands. All we found when we checked into a new club was a tiny dance floor that doubled as the stage.

Almost invariably our preparation for the act had to be done outside the club. We had to be totally self-contained. And then we had to come in and dazzle people at closer range than illusionsists had ever worked before. And we weren't on and off in the typical fifteen minutes. We did a half hour act, what was then considered a full-scale show. We did the metamorphosis, we had the rabbits and doves, I swallowed razor blades, did sleight of hand, mental telepathy, and I had dancing canes. My opening illusion was a routine in which I produced birds, a cane, birds, a cane—back and forth. To accommodate the idea of being so self-contained, I added a broom illusion where Roy was levitated while holding on to a broom.

There were a few other things we hadn't figured on either: like how difficult it was to travel from town to town with a large wild animal. We stayed in bed and breakfasts, and we soon realized we couldn't just walk up to the front desk with a cheetah on a leash. So I would go in first to see if two rooms were available. After being told there was a vacancy, I would then ask if the management minded that we had a cat.

"Oh, of course not, no problem."

I would then explain to the concierge that ours was a rather large cat, using expressive hand movements to show it was seriously big. The concierge would think it was some funny exaggeration and laugh, and I would chuckle along with her, all the while giving Roy the sign to come in. By the time he strolled in with Chico on a leash, the poor concierge was so stunned she couldn't think of what to do.

Then there was the insecurity of not knowing from month to month, sometimes week to week, where we were going to perform next. It was evident to me very early that this was a less than desirable way of life, so we supplemented our touring with the occasional ten-day engagement on a German cruise ship.

In the back of my head I knew that the only place we could get a long-term contract

Look for the magic around you . . .
When we saw the cleaning ladies swinging their brooms at Bremen's Astoria Theater,
it inspired us to do something in their honor.

in all Europe with a specialty act like ours was at the Lido or the Folies-Bergère in Paris. This, of course, was my dream.

R*oy*

What we packed into those months of touring! The highs, the lows, the drama of surviving. When I look back, it seems impossible that we were able to do what we did in such a short time; it seems like years' worth of living.

The first thing we needed to survive was a car to drive our little act—our whole world, really—around Europe. I made an appeal to my aunt Paula, who was willing to buy us a car but reminded me that I needed a driver's license first. So before I left the ship, I alternated between studying for my driver's test and feebly typing—with two fingers—letters to clubs seeking an engagement.

I got my driver's license, and Aunt Paula asked me what kind of car I wanted. I knew exactly. A big Citroën MX 600—so ugly that it was beautiful, so powerful that when you got on the highway, it just flew like an airplane. I chose the model with a chauffeur's window so Chico could have the back to himself.

With our ever-growing menagerie loaded up in the back of the car and our metamorphosis trunk strapped to the roof, Siegfried and I made our way around Germany and eventually to Switzerland, Monte Carlo, Madrid, and Paris. All odds were against us. But in order to find out if you can swim, you have to jump into deep water. Well, we did just that, and to make it a little more interesting, we swam against the current.

For starters, there was the financial dilemma. The pay was bad in these clubs, and the cost of room, board, and feeding our animals left us with next to nothing. We were actually starving. We played a couple of engagements where the salary at eighty marks was a little better—not enough to live, not enough to die.

Feeding Chico was the biggest expense because he required meat without any fat. So while Chico was eating sirloin, Siegfried and I ate burned potatoes. Though we could afford the potatoes, we couldn't spare the money for the butter to sauté them. And then I took pity on a stray cat, and we needed food for her.

We frequented pawnshops a lot during those early months. We could have appealed to our families for a little help, but they were so dead set against our going into show business that we didn't want to ask for assistance. For them, what we were doing was no different from being fire-eaters in a traveling circus. And we were too proud. If we were going to call and tell them anything about our career, it would be to say that we had made it.

Our first turning point after the Astoria came when we succeeded in getting an engagement at the Hansa Theater in Hamburg, the other surviving vaudeville house and the only one left today. It had a very good reputation as a showcase for agents and talent scouts. An agent saw us and booked us for Switzerland.

When I look back on these days, the words to describe us are "earnest" and "honest." We had that youthful seriousness mixed in with a naïveté so that when we encountered people in the "business" who weren't particularly desirable, we were always a little shocked. From day one Siegfried and I had principles and standards; no matter how desperate we were to survive and succeed, we didn't want to compromise ourselves or get pushed around. Wherever we went it was in honesty and with a deep sincerity in what

Shhh . . . remember, the magician never reveals his secret!

we were doing. And because of this, we found ourselves in situations that were real eye-openers.

I remember once before making our way to Switzerland, we had landed what I thought was a very good month-long engagement at a well-known nightclub in Berlin called Eden-Saloon, run by a notorious Berlin playboy, Rolf Eden, who drove a Mercedes sports car and always had a girl on each arm. We had been told that this was *the* place in Berlin to perform. It had ballet, dancing horses, everything you could imagine. So we signed the contract thinking it was going to be like a German version of the Paris Lido.

The drive to Berlin was a nightmare in itself. The route I took was all along the border of East and West Germany and so bleak, so depressing it seemed as if the war were still in progress; I swore I'd never drive that road again. When we reached Berlin, we had trouble at the border, so we arrived a day late for our engagement.

We immediately went to look at the club. A total disappointment. Much smaller than we thought. Not at all the way it had been described. In the window there was a photo of Siegfried and me with Chico, but we were practically cut off on the photo so it was mostly of our cheetah. The caption called him not Chico but Chito, and it read something like "Come see the ferocious Chito; he will dazzle you. . . ." Nothing about us. It was sheer sensationalism. And there we were, two clean-cut young performers with our trunk and box of dreams.

Once we looked at the stage, it was obvious that dancing horses or anything else as elaborate as that couldn't perform here, for it was hardly what you could call a stage. The club had obviously wanted to sell us on the idea of appearing. The stage was the tiniest one we'd ever been asked to work on. In order to get on and off it, we had to go through the audience. Our preparation was done in the house entrance of the club next door.

The place was nothing more than a sleazy striptease joint where all the hookers and the so-called society of Berlin came for a laugh. It was the epitome of a decadent Berlin nightclub. And because Berlin was divided and everyone looked or was suspicious, you got all kinds of strange people.

I'll never forget the striptease act before we went on. She was a well-known French stripper, exceptionally beautiful and the star attraction of the cabaret. One night I walked by her dressing room as she was taking off her costume. I stopped dead in my tracks: She was a transvestite.

Siegfried and I certainly didn't fit the bill for that place. The owner had been right about one thing: It was the in spot. The place was packed every night. Because our act was so different, we turned out to be the toast of the city. And we learned something incredibly positive: the power to transmit our own karma to the audience. With our magic and mysticism, we were an effective, if brief, contrast to Berlin's corrupt spirit.

In addition to performing at Eden-Saloon, we did matinee performances at the Titania Palace and Urania Palace. These were the two remaining grand theaters of Berlin, left over from the city's golden prewar era of entertainment.

It didn't matter how good our karma was when it was time to get our paycheck, for the owner of the place was such a pain. No sooner had we arrived in Berlin than Chico got an abscess in his tooth and was so sick he couldn't perform. All he could do was rest his head against the coal-burning stove in my room, so the heat could soothe his aching mouth. After a couple of days the abscess burst, and he was right back at work.

When we got our paychecks, I noticed the owner had deducted the two days that Chico didn't perform. I confronted the owner, who said that he had paid us for the first performance we missed because of the problems at the border. Thank you, I told him, but that's irrelevant; in my view, we perform, you pay. If he didn't want to pay us for the performance we missed, that was fine. But he owed us for the nights the cheetah was sick because Siegfried and I still went on. Not wanting to give in totally to my demands, he paid us for the two days and took out for the day we missed. Okay. The important thing was that I got my point across, that I had no problem confronting this big shot of Berlin. It was good practice. Siegfried and I have never let anyone take advantage of us.

I'm not sure if that kind of discipline—sticking to your principles, standing up for what you believe, never lowering yourself—can be taught. I think it's instinctive. For us I do believe it came out of a deep love of what we were doing. Our show, our talent, our dreams, our goals of succeeding in show business and performing were our whole lives.

And thirty years later, nothing has changed.

Siegfried

We've always had a sense of who we are. There were opportunities that came along we turned down because we didn't want to compromise. We didn't want to give in to what the public was used to seeing at the time. We wanted to be who we were.

But believe me, when you're practically starving, it's hard to turn down something that looks like an easy ticket to success and security.

While performing in Hamburg, we met the great Kalanag's wife, Gloria, who had been his stage assistant. Kalanag had died, and Gloria was looking for a young illusionist basically to follow in his footsteps. She owned an entire train filled with all his props, costumes, everything from his stage shows; she wanted to find someone to become the second Kalanag. She had seen us perform and thought we were the only illusionists worthy of this opportunity. Promoters had rented a castle outside Munich where we could go and rehearse and perfect the dead master's show. We would inherit everything.

This was, on every level, a splendid opportunity.

I couldn't accept the offer. As uncertain as our future was, I understood that Kalanag was the great Kalanag, and Siegfried and Roy were something else entirely. I admired Kalanag greatly, but I could never envision myself as him because I had by this time developed my own style as an illusionist. Kalanag was from another era. We didn't want to do his acts; we wanted to develop our own and a style for our time.

Despite all the negatives at the time, there was one thing in our favor: We had no competition. The only illusionists left were the big names who had elaborate stage acts or were connected to large circuses. Mostly there were magicians who manipulated with cards and coins and produced birds. Because of the handicap of working surrounded, illusionists didn't perform in clubs.

It seemed strange, but our only competition was ourselves.

Roy

From Germany we made our way to Switzerland, where we played in a series of small clubs. Our first significant engagement was in Geneva at the Moulin Rouge, a well-known nightclub there—again, in all reality, a sophisticated striptease joint. And we still had to break up the act into fifteen-minute segments.

By then we had been on the road for a good eighteen months, and we were getting a bit desperate and worried that something wasn't going to gel. At that time I had the responsibility of securing the engagements—writing letters, sending photos and press clippings, approaching different booking agents to see if something was available in a particular club. So far I had done a good job of getting advance bookings, but after Geneva I hadn't been able to line anything up. Though we had sort of built up a minor reputation on the club circuit, we were financially still barely making it from month to month.

While we were playing at the Moulin Rouge, Switzerland's world-renowned Circus Knie came to Geneva and was playing right across the street from the club. Famous for its brilliant animal acts, this circus was, and still is, one of the best in the world.

By now the Lido in Paris seemed far beyond us. Though that was Siegfried's dream, it wasn't necessarily mine. I wanted to think of some way we could be bigger and be more of our own instead of a small act in a revue. To me the Circus Knie might be the answer.

Though I had never harbored any hopes, even as a child, to run away with a circus—unlike my brother, who actually did run away with one—my imagination ran wild when I saw the Knie move in across the street. I pictured this magnificent scenario of Siegfried and me taking over the entire circus. One elephant—an animal I had always wanted since I was small—could bring in our props while I rode in on another. A cheetah in a nightclub was special, but I envisioned Siegfried vanishing lions, tigers, and horses.

I was realistic enough to know that it wouldn't be an easy task. No circus, particularly one that traveled, was going to commit to something like that quickly. It took a little time to convince Siegfried of my wild plan, but finally I was able to coax him into going to see the owner, Freddy Knie.

No one had ever asked me that question before.

"Well, Madame Pashe, I've never worked in a place as beautiful as this. I have no idea. Whatever you think is best."

"Oh, I'm going to give you the best light you could ever think of."

From our opening night, we had great success at the Cabaret Tabaris. Right after the premiere Madame Pashe told us she was leaving for Monaco. "I'm happy I can leave knowing how wonderful you are," she said, "because when I get there, I'd like to recommend you to perform in the casino at Monte Carlo."

It was this engagement in Monte Carlo that really was our big breakthrough. While playing there, we were invited to perform at the Sporting Club for the annual Red Cross gala in the presence of Prince Rainier and Princess Grace of Monaco, la Gala des Rois. To think that in less than nine months we had gone from walking in off the street into striptease joints to performing for Grace Kelly—from hookers to royalty! You can imagine what that meant to us. The program included some of the best performers in Europe at the time. Among them were Charles Aznavour, Mireille Mathieu, who was the young toast of France and considered the next Piaf, and the famous Bentley Girls, a feast to the living eye, none of whom was under six feet.

That night is still vivid in my memory. From backstage I looked through the curtains, past the gilded balconies with the velvet drapes. I had never seen so much glamour and sophistication. The beauty of the women, the jewels they were wearing, the men in white tie and tails that were encrusted with stars and medals. I could see them all waiting for the performance to begin: Grace Kelly, Sophia Loren, Cary Grant, Maria Callas, and Elizabeth Taylor, to name a few. A chill ran through my body. I began to shake and perspire. I had never been that nervous or scared in my life. It wasn't really stage fright, but more the thought of performing in so elegant an atmosphere before people whom I admired. I felt so out of place. How could Siegfried out of Rosenheim live up to this evening?

This was not the first time, nor would it be the last time, I experienced this. It is in a sense all part of what we do. But the feelings of inadequacy always wash away the minute the curtain goes up. Like an electric shock, the spotlight hits me, I get the feel of the audience, and something magical happens. That night in Monte Carlo it went beyond magic.

The performance was flawless. The audience was cheering; our fifteen-minute performance got the only standing ovation. It was the perfect blend, performing our magic but at the same time projecting charisma as a performer. Until now my inspirations had been people like Edith Piaf, Maurice Chevalier, Sammy Davis, Jr., and Frank Sinatra. I had watched and studied them. The moment performers like those walk onstage, something clicks, and it's magical: The audience and the performer come together as one.

It was a different kind of magic that Roy and I were doing, but we wanted to create the same degree of feeling and texture in our performance. Because the months on the road had prevented us from creating new illusions, we had really devoted ourselves to achieving that other level of magic within the craft.

When we performed at Monte Carlo's Gala des Rois—the singular form, roi, means king in French—it became the namesake for Roy. What a title to live up to!

So there we were on the stage in Monte Carlo with some of the biggest names in show business cheering us. What I had experienced by watching the great ones, I now felt inside me.

 Roy

There was one other climax to the evening.

In the middle of this event there were fireworks outside. It was our good fortune that our act followed them. In the Sporting Club at the back of the stage there was a curtain and behind that an enormous glass cathedral window. It was through this window that the audience watched the fireworks display. When that was over, the curtain was drawn, and we came out. By the time we hit the stage, the audience was already on such a high that our speed and excitement sent them over the top.

Naturally our grand finale was the metamorphosis. At the end of the illusion Chico appeared out of the trunk. He was supposed to jump on top of it and stay there while we took our bows. But the sounds of the fireworks and the screaming of the audience had all been a bit too much for him. He flew out of the trunk, and instead of jumping on top of it, Chico stood in the middle of the stage, stared at everyone, and made his exit through the audience, prancing down the entire length of the Sporting Club of Monte Carlo. Past Prince Rainier, past Grace Kelly, past Sophia Loren, his tail gently brushing their legs and purring all the way.

You always have to make something good out of something bad, right? I pretended it was a part of the act and followed right behind him, waving boldly to the stunned audience. At the time a cheetah was no different to people from a lion or a tiger, so it was an unusually exotic and thrilling moment even for a sophisticated audience like this to have a cheetah walk right by.

I had no idea how I was going to get backstage. When I got to the back of the club, I took the first door I found. Finding myself in the kitchen, I made my way back to the dressing room. By then Siegfried was charging after me, ready to kill me. But I couldn't do anything about what had happened, could I?

Siegfried feared that Chico had killed our success; actually he made it flourish. As it happened, our finale was the highlight of the evening. The next day, the headlines in the newspaper read GALA DES ROIS, SIEGFRIED AND ROY, THE NEW KINGS. The event was picked up by the press all over Europe, and it made the tide turn for us.

Another change, the name of the act, occurred. Until this time we were Siegfried and Partner. Though Uwe was my middle name, it was the one I always used. My first name, Roy, when translated into French, means "king." With the success of our Monte Carlo performance, I decided to use Roy as my name. Quite a name to live up to! It was shortly after this that we became Siegfried and Roy.

Siegfried

The kind of audience we were performing for that night was a tough one. At that level they'd seen the best. To have a standing ovation and the stars coming backstage to tell us how wonderful we were, well, it was a total boost to our confidence. It made me realize we had something special.

While Roy was busy escorting Chico out of the club and I was charging after him, running after me was a man who had been in the audience and was so ecstatic by our performance he wanted to make a deal with us right on the spot. Daniel Marouani, the biggest impresario on the Côte d'Azur, offered us a two-contract deal to play at the prestigious Hôtel Négresco in Nice and then at the Passaboga in Madrid.

I was thrilled. I knew if we were well received in Nice, we could play anywhere, and that would be our ticket to the Lido in Paris.

Roy

It's difficult to write about our success without sounding self-serving. After we played in Monte Carlo and then Nice, the Passaboga in Madrid was a small nightclub with much less grandeur. The conditions were ridiculous. The dressing rooms were one floor above the stage, so we had to carry our props down. But it did have a charm, and it was the main nightclub address in Madrid.

Living in Madrid was a total delight. I adored it. After the rigid Swiss and German way of doing things, I loved the Latin temperament, the colorful personalities, the constant eye rolling that made every situation seem like high drama, and the passion the Spaniards put into everyday life. Yes, I was definitely in my element there. I even got very Spanish myself.

At one point during this engagement we got a telegram from René Fraday, the artistic

your act will be sensational zere, zee way how you do your doves—ah! such style, such panache, and zee cheeee-tah! Well, it weeeelll be ze toast of Paris!"

Siegfried told him he needed to speak with me. So he called me from the house phone and told me the whole story.

Right away I got defensive. Siegfried was always telling me, and still does, that criticism is helpful, it makes you better. Personally I've never been able to be so accepting.

"No, don't give in," I said. "Let him suffer."

Fraday asked Siegfried to come with him to his hotel for a little nightcap, so they could discuss things out of the atmosphere of a striptease joint. Again, a put-down of everything that was not his!

They went to his hotel. He explained in glorified colors what Paris could do for us. But just as they walked into the lobby—as if we had paid someone to do it—there were three typical old American ladies with blue rinse hair, little strands of pearls, and mink stoles. They all recognized Siegfried.

"Oh, you're the magician. Oh, my God, you're so handsome! You're more handsome than you are onstage. You and your partner are terrific. Have you ever performed in America? You should! Why do you want to do this in Europe? You're absolutely tailor-made for Las Vegas. We go there all the time, and you would be fantastic there. We love the animals. Give our love to your partner."

Siegfried could not have had a better setup.

I never met René Fraday. Siegfried called me after the meeting at the hotel to ask what we should do. By that time Tony Azzie had called and requested that the minute we closed at the Passaboga we go to Paris and do one performance for the owners of the Folies-Bergère before we signed the contract.

I told Siegfried that as long as we had to do one show at the Folies, why not go look at the Lido and compare them? I added that regardless of our decision, *I still wanted to go to Las Vegas first.*

Siegfried went back and told René Fraday that whatever we decided to do, we still wanted to go to Las Vegas for three months.

"Oh, zis terrible. If you do this, you'll ruin your career."

In short, more of the same.

"Well, we will see you in Paris in one week," Siegfried continued, "and we'll come see the Lido show."

"What are you saying, 'See zee Lido show'? Zee Lido does not audition for an act."

We finished our engagement in Madrid, loaded up the Citroën, and drove all night in order to get to Paris in time for the next evening's performance of the Folies. On the outskirts of Paris we stopped at a gas station to change into our costumes. We arrived an hour before the show started, met the owner, went across the street to a café for a Campari and soda, and went onstage.

To judge by the audience's response—three curtain calls—and the dancers and stage-hands applauding us from the wings, we knew we had gone over big.

We got the final approval from the owner, who said he definitely wanted us for Las Vegas and then for a year after that in Paris. Of course, we didn't want to sign the contract until we saw the Lido. So we stalled one more time and told him we would give him a decision tomorrow because we had a meeting with the general director of the Lido.

"Zee Lido? *Non, mais non, pas de Lido! Ce n'est pas possible.*"

As you can see, everybody was saying bad things about everyone else.

On to the Lido.

It often happens that when you've been building something up in your head for so long, you're bound to be disappointed. Don't get me wrong, it was wonderful, but with Siegfried, who also had never seen it, talking about it for so many years, my expectations were too great. This was the old Lido, not the one that exists today. The stage was just a dance floor that would rise. The audience sat crowded at little tables. The waiters had to step on your feet just to get through. It did have a definite ambience, though, which is as important as the work space.

Regardless of the disappointment, we knew the Lido was far more prestigious than the Folies-Bergère. After the show we met with Pierre Louis-Guèrin, who was the epitome of what you think of as the general director of the Lido. He had snow white hair, a crisp white starched shirt, and a white tie that looked starched as well, and unlike René Fraday, he exuded charisma. We met with him and Fraday in his office, told him how much we enjoyed the place, but said we really wanted to go to Las Vegas first.

For Monsieur Louis-Guèrin, that was a scandal. They were so upset. They said it would be okay if we started at the Lido first, then made a contract with them to perform in their show at the Stardust in Las Vegas, but the other way around was unacceptable. Of course, they were thinking of the 10 percent cut they would get if they sent us to Vegas.

"Well, if you go with the Folies in Vegas, you will never work again in Paris. Never. Don't even bother coming to zee Lido when you return."

And with that we went to Las Vegas.

ACT FOUR

Round about what is, lies a whole mysterious world of might be . . .

—HENRY WADSWORTH LONGFELLOW

In our dressing room at the Tropicana Hotel—ready to hit the stage for our Las Vegas debut. Those pinup girls, however, almost made us lose our concentration.

Roy

The plane descended, and I looked out the window for my first glimpse of the entertainment capital of the world. But what was this? It looked like a hick town; all I could see were a few houses and a sprinkling of lights. *Oh my God!* I thought. *What have I done?* Then the pilot announced that we were passing over Bakersfield and would soon be landing in Las Vegas.

When we finally reached Las Vegas, I had an instant love for the place. And believe me, in 1967, it was not the Las Vegas it is today. The airport was situated on a tiny piece of desert. The Las Vegas Strip consisted of a lot fewer hotels than today. Still, with the names of the greatest entertainers of the day lit up in neon and the twinkling hotel marquees set against the backdrop of a pink desert sky and the mountains, Las Vegas was quite a sight for my German eyes.

I had envisioned Las Vegas as this grand, exotic, almost tropical place with a touch of the *Arabian Nights*. In the spirit of grandeur, I arrived with not one but two cheetahs—Chico and our new addition, Simba, who was so adorable and affectionate that it was an instant, instant love affair. And to fit in with what I thought was the tropical mood of the place, I brought along some flamingos from my uncle's zoo. I must have looked like a Bedouin, laden down with my menagerie and all my worldly possessions.

You know the old saying, "If anything can go wrong, it will?" Well, our metamorphosis trunk had done a disappearing act and didn't make it to Las Vegas. Without it, we

Roy

After getting the French almost as well trained as my animals, we were the toast of Paris. We liked it. Soon we even got used to it.

One night after the show Pierre Louis-Guèrin asked that we meet with him. He had a proposal for us. In six months he wanted us to go to Las Vegas and open the new Lido show at the Stardust Hotel. I was thrilled with this proposition. If we could have opened in Vegas immediately, I would have boarded the next plane.

Then I turned to Siegfried, and there I saw a face as long as the Amazon telling Monsieur Guèrin we would have to think about it. I was surprised by his attitude. *Oh, but he's being quite the businessman,* I thought. *How clever. This time he'll get the French to pay back the fifty francs.*

Siegfried didn't say a word after that. When the meeting was over, we headed for a little café on the Champs-Élysées. After settling in with two espressos and a cognac, I asked what the problem was.

"I don't want to go."

Well, that was certainly direct and to the point. I was in shock. "Why, Siegfried, what are you saying? This is the greatest thing that could happen. America! I love it. It's the greatest country in the world. We'll be conquering it all the way. Please, Siegfried, we've got to go."

My plea didn't convince him.

"Oh, Roy, you're such a dreamer," he said. "Remember how difficult it was at the Tropicana, how many problems we had. They want to see only big stars. You know how much talent is in that country. They aren't waiting for a little German act like ours. And anyway, all there is to Vegas is the Strip and the desert. What kind of a life is that? You want to sacrifice everything we have built up here for a shot in the sky?"

On and on he went. After ten years together, I knew the routine. Siegfried was against the new idea; I was all for it. I would have to plead, coax, manipulate, and threaten, and finally he would come around. In fact, by the time he made up his mind, he would think it was his idea in the first place. Thank God I'm not in politics.

Well, after a lot of my promising him the world and convincing him that we had to try it, we owed it to ourselves, even if we failed, Siegfried finally agreed.

I could have jumped the moon. America! Show business! Here we come!

In order to make Siegfried happy and ready to face Las Vegas, I decided we would leave the Lido three months earlier. I wanted Siegfried to have a nice long vacation in Bavaria.

It was a good thought.

Not too long after we decided to go to Las Vegas, Wolf Kochman, an American producer, was in the audience, and Francis Brunn, a good friend and the most stylish juggler in the world, brought him backstage to meet us. Wolf, an extremely nice man of German descent, was in partnership with a director-choreographer called Barry Ashton, and he offered us a one-year contract for the Barry Ashton Casino Royal show in San Juan, Puerto Rico.

We explained we had only three months before we opened in Las Vegas. Undeterred, he said they'd be happy to book us for those three months. And because there was only one show a night and a day off a week, it would be more like a paid vacation for us than work.

We weren't even sure where Puerto Rico was and what language was spoken. This time, though, I didn't have to persuade Siegfried of anything.

Our mutual enthusiasm didn't falter when we reached San Juan. From the window of the plane we gawked at a postcard-blue sky, ivory white beaches, and graceful palm trees. Then we stepped out of the plane into the tropical lush environment; the air was warm and moist and fragrant.

"Boy, this is paradise," I remarked to Siegfried.

Wishful thinking.

As we cleared our personal luggage through customs, Siegfried and I, like good magicians, disappeared the doves. He carried a basket with only the four understudies, which we'd brought with us in case there was a problem with quarantine.

Amazingly enough, there was none. The customs officials were charming and respectful—so pleasant, in fact, that Siegfried asked if the four doves in the basket were a problem. "Ah, *la paloma, no tiene problema,*" we were told. Siegfried was so taken by their laid-back Caribbean nature that he decided to return the hospitality. He made the rest of the fifteen doves magically reappear into the basket.

At this point I headed for the cargo department to deal with the cheetahs, props, and costumes. While I was there, Siegfried rushed up to me in an absolute panic. Apparently, just after he got all the doves back in the basket and passed through customs, the doves—happy to be free again—started to coo.

At the same time there was a shift change. A new official heard the sound and asked

Imagination is more

ACT FIVE

important than information.

—ALBERT EINSTEIN

R_{oy}

In 1973, when our three-year contract was up for renewal, the Stardust showed us how much it wanted us to stay by offering us a much more lucrative deal. We knew better than to accept it. Once again we were no longer challenged; our imaginations had moved far ahead of what we were able to achieve.

We were not short of offers.

Edgar Lansbury, a Broadway producer, approached us with his new venture, *The Magic Show*. Naturally we were flattered but we were realistic. Siegfried and I felt we weren't ready for what we thought Broadway required: not just magic but singing and dancing as well. We had flourished in revues, and we simply couldn't envision ourselves doing magic within the context of a musical. Our refusal was the gain for a young Canadian magician who had come to America to study magic on a grant from his government and had become our friend: Doug Henning.

Doug was little and wiry—elflike. As soon as we met him, we were charmed. He was a great talker, and with his wide, toothy grin and childlike happiness, he was perfect for the role of the young magician in *The Magic Show*, and the show made Doug's career.

As for us? On the heels of our sucess in Las Vegas, we accepted an offer that to some might have looked like the wrong choice. Our friends in Puerto Rico, Wolf Kochman and Barry Ashton, invited us back to their show at the Americana Hotel. It would be a yearlong engagement with us getting star billing and the plum position as closing act in the revue. There was also an additional bonus: one show a night and one day off a week. So Puerto Rico would be like a well-deserved vacation for us as well as a chance to develop some new illusions.

We knew we weren't taking a risk by leaving Las Vegas for a year. If we kept our options open, we were certain we'd be offered something exciting. Before we left for Puerto Rico, Donn Arden, who had been the director and choreographer of the Stardust/ Lido, informed us he was leaving the show and was negotiating with MGM to stage a huge spectacular for the long-planned but as yet unbuilt MGM Grand Hotel. If everything worked out, he wanted us to be a part of the show.

Our act in Puerto Rico was the same one we'd been doing for three years, except that along the way we had begun to expand our menagerie. We arrived with Sabu, a black panther, and our leopard, Sasha, and, in addition to Sahra, we now had Radscha, a 650-pound Sumatran tiger. Sadly, both Chico and Simba had died of kidney and liver disease; their replacements for the metamorphosis were the leopard and the panther. All of them were appearing and disappearing nightly.

Several months into our stint in Puerto Rico we got the call from Donn Arden to say he had finalized his contract as producer-director of a show called *Hallelujah Hollywood* for the MGM Grand Hotel. Drawing on the massive archives of the MGM studios, Arden would pay tribute to the studio's heyday, showcasing many of the great songs and moments from the MGM classic movie musicals. The show would be a lavish *Ziegfeld Follies* type of production featuring dance ensembles, dazzling chorus girls, singers, and comedians. Arden wanted us to be the closing act, coming on just before the grand finale.

It didn't take us long to agree to join Arden. His adventure was just what we were looking for.

I knew right away what we should do. If we could organize it, it would be the ultimate statement for the new show.

I've always related to my tigers and panthers and leopards, I guess because they're loners, and to some degree I am, too—a happy one, mind you. But although tigers, panthers, and leopards have always given me something I can see in myself, I had always dreamed of having a lion. As the lion is the MGM symbol, I thought this would be a perfect occasion to have one, to pay tribute. With a lot of persuasion, I convinced Siegfried.

Dr. Marty Dinnes, our veterinarian and friend for twenty-five years, located a full-grown big-maned African lion with a supposedly fantastic disposition. As you can imagine, after having been on an airplane, then waiting a day in the New York airport and trying to break out of his transport box, he arrived wild, with no intention of accepting my human lead. Leo was a magnificent animal, but even more difficult to handle than a green lion out of the wilderness.

I built an enclosure outside my living room and bedroom so he could see me at all times and I could spend every free minute with him. Before we could even begin to work with him, I had to get him to regain his trust in human beings. That took three months of constant daily contact. By this time we were getting closer to our return date to Las Vegas. We wanted to incorporate him into the show in Puerto Rico so he'd be ready for his big debut.

The illusion called for me to enter an empty cage, a cloth came over the cage, and in

**Roy in Puerto Rico posing for a Spanish magazine with Radscha,
a Sumatran Tiger**

*Little did I know that minutes later Radscha and I would have a brush with death. Siegfried had
forgotten to close the front door of the photographer's studio. Soon after Radscha and I descended
the staircase, a high wind outside slammed a window shutter, which startled my tiger. As I held
his leash, he bolted straight out the front door and at top speed landed us in the middle of a busy
four-lane highway. It was only because of my guardian angel that we weren't run over.*

Wet n' wild
Leo takes the plunge! A rare photo of a lion embracing a new element—water.

milk, expecting to find babies or to learn that Sasha had killed them because of the circumstances. Nothing. All Sasha did was hug me on contact, relieved that we were on the ground.

From New York we had to fly to Los Angeles and from there take a plane to Vegas. Siegfried decided to stay in New York for a few days to see some Broadway shows, so I flew alone to L.A. with our props and animals. Again, in L.A., the same thing. I was armed with bottles of milk—but no new arrivals. I was anxious to keep moving and get home, but there were no planes until the next morning.

As far as I was concerned, my animals had already spent too much time in transport boxes, so I hired an enormous truck with a driver, loaded everything up, and got ready to go. One problem: The driver informed me it was against company rules for me to ride

Roy with Sabu in Puerto Rico, 1973

*My black panther, Sabu, is extremely demanding of my attention. If I don't greet him
first in the morning, he ignores me all day. Whenever I'm on vacation
he refuses to eat if I don't telephone him daily.*

*Sabu's jealously knows no boundaries. In the house I once rented in Puerto Rico
I had a black-and-white marble-floored bedroom with a king-size water bed—a domain
that one mighty black panther found delicious.*

*After our opening at the Americana Hotel in San Juan, I invited all the two-legged dancing
beauties back to the house for a glass of champagne. After a few loud laughs and clinking of
glasses, we were interrupted by violent noises from the bedroom. In a fit of jealousy, Sabu went
berserk and destroyed the room, ripping open the water bed, which then flooded the party.
Age has not mellowed him.*

121

Michael called, we came.
Michael Jackson had asked us to design some illusions that he could perform in his world tour.
We arrived in Pensacola, Florida, and went immediately to the stadium to show him how they
worked. After mastering the illusions, he was so relieved that he whipped up a special vegetarian
dinner for us. We had flown three thousand miles and having had only a Glenlivet on the rocks
and a few peanuts, Roy couldn't hide his disappointment. "Sorry, Michael, I'm just like
my tigers—carnivorous!"

clever as we should have been. For the Grand, star billing meant that *if* another act was ever mentioned, we would be above the other acts, but we would never be above the title of the show. The agreement was phrased in such a way that . . .

Roy

. . . it gave us ab-so-lute-ly . . . *nothing*. And I mean *nothing*. Aside from the contract there was, in the end, an enormous irony about the entire setup. One of the reasons why we left the Stardust was the lack of stage space we had for our performance. We were attracted by the MGM offer when we heard about the size of the stage that was being built. Naturally we thought we would have more space. So we arrived at the MGM, thinking we had overcome many obstacles.

Wrong.

We ended up in front of the curtain, and because of the massive movie studio-type sceneries and sets, we had *less* space than we had at the Stardust. To make more room, Arden also eliminated the orchestra pit and put the musicians in the basement. They watched the show on a TV monitor; the music was piped into the theater. For us, that wasn't a whole lot different from taped music at the Lido in Paris.

So there we were transforming, appearing, disappearing, and reappearing our 650-pound lion, our 450-pound tiger, a leopard, a panther, in addition to all that, Siegfried and I had six costume changes—all this done in an area sixteen feet square.

Nevertheless, we continued to operate on the belief that we had made the right career move. If we had been able to make changes at the Stardust, surely as the closing act at the MGM we'd have the freedom to add to our act. And whatever happened, we thought the show probably wouldn't run more than three years. Considering it was the hottest show on the strip, I don't know why we were so confident.

Hallelujah Hollywood actually ran for seven years.

Siegfried

We played the standard two shows a night, three on weekends, no day off with only a yearly two-week vacation. It was after our second year when we went away that we realized how important we were to the show. You see, when an act goes on vacation,

Ali, one of our spotted lep-jags

An extremely rare species, with the beauty and agility of a leopard and the power and strength of a jaguar, this breed is too smart for its own good. We call this creature "a living bullet." But what do you expect when your godfather is Muhammad Ali?

the show still plays; it just has a temporary replacement. Apparently during our time off the managers were swamped with complaints from the audience that had come to the show specifically to see us. The complaint was so big they had to put a sign in front of the theater saying: SIEGFRIED AND ROY ARE NOT APPEARING TONIGHT. Because of that, they got a great many cancellations.

Upon hearing about this, we thought we had some power to negotiate for more time, stage space, and a new illusion.

A day off from the show
It's nice to have poolside friends who don't mind when you splash water on them.

Roy

Quite the contrary. *Hallelujah Hollywood* was a long show, already running overtime; there was no way we could add anything else, and every inch of space was used to make the set changes backstage. Without realizing it, we had dug our own grave. But to the outside world, and to the MGM, we were a huge hit.

They would give us something: more money. That's always great, but in the end it didn't give us the satisfaction we wanted; our creativity was at a standstill.

And from this point on things began to sour.

Poor Siegfried became inwardly and outwardly miserable. He began to feel imprisoned. His ulcers started acting up. Depression set in, and, once again, insomnia, which he cured with Valium. As a result, he wasn't himself anymore. He was on remote control.

Siegfried

This was our most stressful situation as a team. Over the years, as Roy and I went from strength to strength, we grew stronger together. But now we thought we might be stifling each other. We had always shared a house; now I moved out, and the only time we saw each other was at show time. There was a point when we actually considered splitting up.

Roy

I thought of going to Reno to start up a grand-scale solo act with elaborate special effects, an army of show girls, and an African elephant—more of a deluxe show than a magic show. The only trouble was I never cared for Reno, so it was a very short-lived idea, a fleeting moment, for I always had a total unwavering belief in the foundation of our partnership. But it's only human to wonder what you would do if you were on your own.

136

Show biz royalty

A special photo taken in the courtyard of the Jungle Palace—five rare variations of the golden tiger family

137

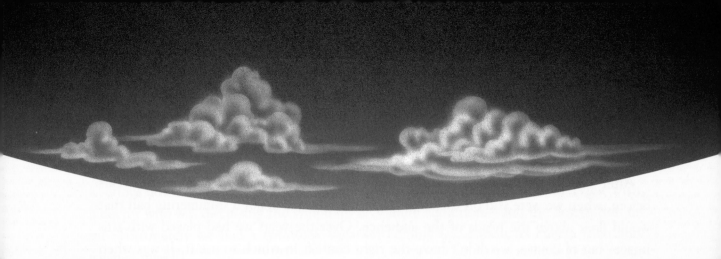

Our devoted friends, Irene and Bill Larsen,
owners of the famous Magic Castle in Los Angeles and
sponsors of the Magicians of the Year Award

With Zsa Zsa Gabor after receiving the Magicians of the Decade Award from
The Academy of Magical Arts in 1992

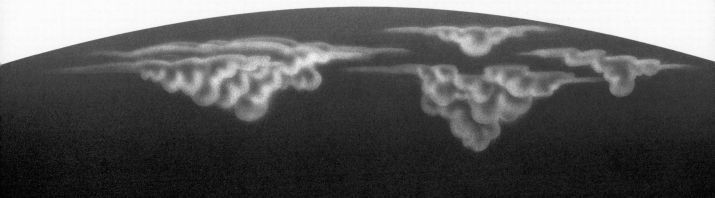

For the last fifteen years we've sponsored the Joe Stevens, Siegfried and Roy Desert Magic Seminar for new talent whose names we hope will become the greats of tomorrow. The most difficult part of this enjoyable few days is trying to decide who gets the award. Magic has come a way since we started and we're continually impressed by the wealth of richly talented, imaginative young magicians.

The magicians' benefit in 1985 for U.S.A. for Africa

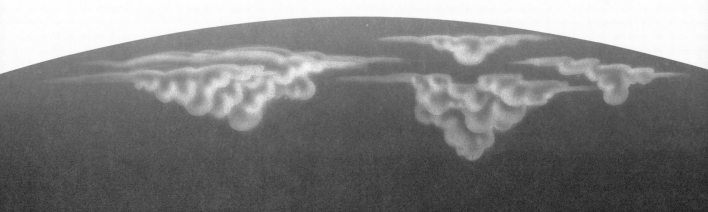

Some of our peers whose talent we respect. Each one has paved the way for a certain style of magic.

John Calvert and Harry Blackstone, Jr.

Channing Pollack

Doug Henning
Hands-on Magic

David Copperfield
*More than a decade ago, we met David's parents, who told us their
teenage son wanted to become a magician. They asked us
if it was possible that he could earn a living doing it. "If he's really determined,
then the magic within himself will find its path," we told them.
It must have been good advice, for he is one of the great magicians of today.*

144

Reverend John Booth—author, magician, magic historian and friend

With Mark Wilson and two of Japan's leaders in the art of magic

Japan's Princess Tenko

Visiting with the Board of Directors of the Desert Magic Seminar —the who's who of the magic world

With Penn and Teller
Penn: "I am the Roy of Penn and Teller."
Teller: "Of course! Because I am the Siegfried."

I AM THE ROY OF Penn + Teller

OF COURSE! BECAUSE I AM the Siegfried

With our personal manager, Bernie Yuman—a star in his own right

As a result of Bernie's artful negotiations on our behalf—from the Stardust/Lido to our *Beyond Belief* show at the Frontier to Japan, Radio City Music Hall, and the Mirage—he has become more than the driving force behind Siegfried and Roy; he's earned the respect of his peers in the industry.

When we were in Germany in 1991 to receive the Bambi—the country's highest media award—for our television special, Siegfried and I were asked by an interviewer what other star did we think would be deserving of the award. Without a moment's thought, Siegfried turned and said, "Our manager, Bernie Yuman."

And to that, I can only say, Bernie, for us you soar as high as the eagle in the sky.

Siegfried

When I look back on how Bernie negotiated the Stardust deal, I'm still amazed. The new owners were so excited to have us that Bernie was able to secure from them all our requests. They agreed to build facilities for our animals, and they did the same thing for Roy and me as well, a dressing room/apartment built just for us.

What we wanted to do in this show was to have our magic enhance the big production. We had full use of the stage and we incorporated the Lido sceneries and backdrops into our half hour. We also wanted to take advantage of all the elements they had to offer, like Bashful, the twenty-seven-year-old five-ton elephant. We wanted to do a vanishing illusion with her. At long last, an elephant for Roy.

Roy

And at long last, we could acknowledge Lynette Chappell and Toney Mitchell for their years of friendship and assistance. We'd wanted to bring them onstage for some time—to us, they both had star quality—but our act had never been long enough to do that.

There are women, and then there are *women*. Lynette is definitely the *most* woman I've ever met. She is gorgeous with an easy go-to-ravishing, and she has a chameleonlike ability to transform herself into many different looks. Because of that, she has given me choices over the years, and my hands are always full.

For me to love a woman, she has to be very feminine. Lynette is definitely a feline. And this quality couldn't be better because she is the surrogate mother to many of my four-legged children.

Our paths crossed when the then–flaming redhead Lynette was the principal dancer in the previous Stardust/Lido show. There was an instant spark, and our relationship developed—second to none—surpassing rain, hail, or high water.

Born in Mombasa, Kenya, Lynette trained as a ballerina with the Royal School of Ballet in London. Because of that, she understood and respected discipline.

Lynette also was a very quick study of our personalities. As she later told us, she figured us out one day during rehearsal. The bandleader was making an absolute mess of a piece

Lynette taking charge of the stage as the Evil Queen in our show at the Mirage

The elegance and grace of Lynette Chappell, our beautiful female star, is no illusion.

of music that didn't seem wildly complicated to us. Siegfried has very little patience for artistic screwups. He banged his hands on the metamorphosis trunk and shouted, "This music is written in twenty-seven languages! Is it possible you don't know *any* of them?" And Lynette, who had never seen a novelty act quite so demanding, said to herself, "Hmm . . . better not mess around with these two."

153

Toney in character as the Chief Acolyte in the Mirage show

Toney in his domain at the Jungle Palace

Well, this is certainly better than pulling rabbits out of a hat.

Four left feet
Our television specials gave us an opportunity to explore new avenues and angles and new illusions—like singing and dancing. Broadway, here we come. You just have to remember, it's not how you start, it's how you finish!

Even Siegfried was amazed that he was able to transform me into a three-foot version of myself. For once, he wasn't worried that I would upstage him.

Frivolous beauty
And the perfect pet. Everyone should have one. Yeah—in a while, crocodile!

Man masters nature
not by force but by
understanding.

—JACOB BRONOWSKI

ACT SIX

Opening night of "Beyond Belief"

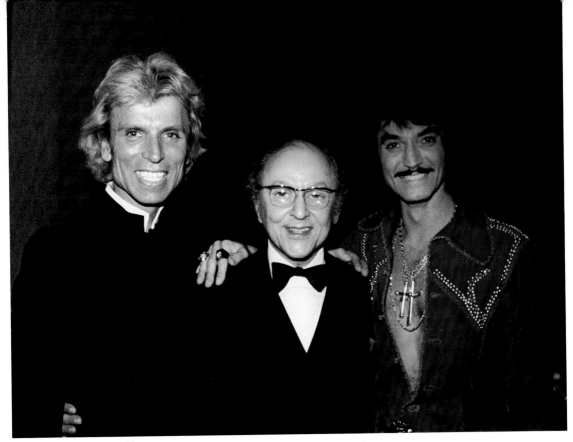

The greatest showman on earth, and our mentor, Irvin Feld

R_{oy}

You would never have known to look at him. Five feet seven, 125 pounds, heavy glasses with bottle-thick lenses—on one hand, Irvin Feld seemed buttoned up and businesslike. But then you looked below the neck, and everything changed. The neckties blinded you, the lining of the vibrantly colored sports jackets matched the ties, and the omnipresent cigar made figure eights in the air. This was the other side of Irvin Feld; this was the greatest showman on earth.

Feld was the kind of man who focused all his energies on you, so it took us awhile to learn his story, which was in its way just as remarkable as ours. He was the son of a struggling Maryland store owner, and from the time he was thirteen, he spent his summers helping support his family. Snake oil, toothpaste, aspirin, rubbing alcohol—it didn't matter what he sold, as long as he could travel on the carnival circuit. Before he knew it, the big top was in his blood.

In 1935, after graduating from high school, Feld was approached by the NAACP to open a pharmacy in the black section of Washington, D.C., which they would finance because the neighborhood was without one. Feld was surprised and happy to get the financial support—and when he opened the pharmacy, he was even happier to add a record department featuring black music. He put speakers in the window that blared the music out onto the street and attracted customers. Within two years, he and his brother, Israel, owned a chain of record stores.

But retailing wasn't for Irvin Feld. He recognized young talent, and he backed it by starting his own label. Feld had the touch: In 1945 a song on his label, "Guitar Boogie," by Arthur Smith and The Crackerjacks, became the first independently produced record ever to sell a million copies.

People like to say that Elvis invented rock and roll. Or maybe it was Chuck Berry or Bill Haley. I think you could make a case that the real originator was Irvin Feld, the first promoter to sense that the big band era was dead and rhythm and blues had arrived. Frank Sinatra had never performed in arenas; Irvin pushed him to do so, with great success. Paul Anka was a fifteen-year-old Canadian when Feld discovered him; overnight he became a teen idol. Fabian, Chubby Checker, Fats Domino, Frankie Avalon, Buddy Holly, the Everly Brothers—Feld found them and booked them and made them household names. And it was Irvin who brought the Beatles to America for the first time.

*S*iegfried

Another promoter might have stopped there and spent the rest of his life in the music business. But Feld had an old itch, and in 1956 he scratched it. It was, of course, the Ringling Brothers and Barnum & Bailey Circus, and what interested Feld was that it was on the verge of going out of business. So in typical Feld style, he wrote John Ringling North a note, analyzing the circus's problems and offering to fix them.

North ignored him. Six months later, when the circus folded, North had to swallow his pride and call Feld. Irvin kept him on hold for a delicious two minutes.

"Do you know who I am?" North bellowed when Feld finally deigned to talk to him.

"Yes," Feld cracked, "you're the guy whose circus closed today."

"I'd like to change that," North said.

"Your circus—how many roustabouts do you hire?"

"Two thousand."

"Do they eat?"

"They do," North said, "and better food than you do."

Feld was unfazed. "So you're in the restaurant business, and you've got a pretty big restaurant, too. Tell me, where do these roustabouts sleep?"

"We provide bunks."

"Oh, so you're in the hotel business, too. Tell me, why do you have the roustabouts to begin with?"

"Because they put up the tent," North said, as though talking to a child.

"Hmm, you're in the construction business as well," mused Feld. And then his voice hardened. "I think you're in too many businesses. If I get you out of the restaurant, hotel, and construction businesses, you may get to stay in the circus business."

That is what North did. He fired the roustabouts, dumped the tent, and cut the payroll fifty thousand dollars in the first week. A month later the circus was back in business, and Feld was its booking agent. And that wasn't all: Knowing that North would try to get rid of him as soon as the circus was profitable again, Feld had inserted an unbreakable clause in his contract that made it endlessly self-renewing.

A decade later Feld owned the circus. Two circuses really, for he divided it into two units—the Red and the Blue—to generate greater revenues. In a style that P. T. Barnum would have envied, the eight-million-dollar deal was ceremoniously sealed in the center of Rome's Colosseum. In addition to the resonant surroundings, there was another hook: North didn't trust paper money, so Feld had to pay his price in gold.

A few years later, in 1971, Irvin sold the circus to Mattel for fifty million dollars. For Irvin it was a deal that got even better when Mattel decided it was too much trouble and sold it back to him eleven years later, for twenty-three million dollars. Irvin Feld was one smart cookie.

R_{oy}

Meeting Irvin and his son, Kenneth, had a tremendous impact on us. Quite simply they changed our lives.

The television specials they produced were a huge success. The shows, particularly the second one, got high ratings, and both were sold all over the world. It's amazing, but we still receive letters from people who tell us they've just seen one of these specials in Brazil, Italy, or France.

It was after the second show that the Felds approached us with another, more permanent offer. Irvin Feld had been following our career since we arrived in Las Vegas. By analyzing our growth pattern, he had a clear vision of what we should be doing. After seeing what we were able to accomplish for the television specials, he convinced us that we had outgrown the Stardust and that we could carry a full-length show by ourselves.

At the same time that Irvin Feld was our key to a new dimension, we also held the key to one of his aspirations.

Siegfried

Las Vegas was the only place that had eluded Irvin as a promoter, a producer, and an impresario for over forty years. In us he saw the potential to realize finally the dream of producing his own show in Las Vegas.

In retrospect, to have our own show was the natural follow-up to the Stardust/Lido. We were getting offers right, left, and center, but it was Irvin Feld who sensed something in us that no one in Las Vegas saw, and to a certain degree, we didn't either: that two Germans could carry a full-length magic spectacle, which we appropriately named *Beyond Belief*.

It was a wild idea, and no one in Las Vegas thought we could pull it off, but we knew that with Feld backing us it could happen.

Roy

The newly founded team of Irvin Feld, Kenneth Feld, and Bernie Yuman went into negotations with the owners of the Frontier hotel, Summa Corporation—the company started by Howard Hughes many years before. And the result was that our team procured the richest contract in the history of Las Vegas. Bingo!

Of course, Irvin being Irvin, it didn't look that way to the Frontier's tough-minded managers. But there was this one little clause . . .

Siegfried

It was an effect built upon an effect, very much like one of our illusions. The Frontier owners hoped we'd do well, but in the back of their minds they envisioned a nice little show with Siegfried and Roy playing there for three years. No one, except for Irvin, Kenneth, and Bernie, imagined that we'd fill the theater twice a night and turn so many people away that it would become necessary to add seating.

Irvin always thought we'd be that successful. And so he got the Frontier to agree that every time it raised the ticket price or added to the seating capacity, we would get an increase on our percentage of the revenues. Instead of three years, we played for seven, the showroom went from 800 to 1,000 seats, and the ticket price from twenty to thirty-five dollars. It didn't take the Frontier long to see the numbers flashing before its eyes.

 Roy

The moment that really cemented our relationship with Irvin wasn't financial. It was a piece of showmanship, pure and simple. The day we were to open at the Frontier, Irvin had arranged a big welcome with a police escort, a red carpet, marching bands, and enough press to make you think the President was arriving. We were overwhelmed, but we were also challenged. How could we top Irvin?

The night before the opening, I got the idea. We would be driven in our new midnight blue Rolls, a present from Irvin, but only to the Vegas airport. From there, the driver would continue on to the hotel while we did . . . something else. At exactly the right time the Rolls pulled up to the Frontier. Television cameras were rolling, three hundred newspaper reporters were there, a band played, a formally attired doorman opened the rear car door. Then came the gasps. Siegfried and Roy were nowhere to be seen.

But we were. You just had to look up to see us. And as we landed in our personalized helicopter, the press went crazy. We scarcely noticed. Our eyes were on Irvin Feld, who was saying over and over again, "I don't believe it, this is the most spectacular arrival in show business."

Through the years, Irvin became something more to us than the producer who believed in us and gave us the opportunity to achieve a new growth pattern. He was our mentor, a father figure. Like a loving parent, he showered us with the confidence that for years Siegfried and I had had to give each other, that no one, not our own family, friends, or business associates, could ever give us.

Irvin saw us on the next level of our career before we ever did. We didn't think of ourselves as stars, but he did, and he used to tell us, "You'll never walk in the shadow of someone else." Yet he was never Irvin to us; he was always Mr. Feld.

It wasn't all roses. As in any real family, we had our share of knockdown disagreements and fits of temper, but in the end he made us grow up and see that no matter how creative you are, you have to protect your gift and treat it like a business. He would always say, "First you crawl, then you walk, then you run like hell." You can't disagree with that.

Siegfried

Most producers tend to leave a show alone once they're certain it's in smooth running order. Not Mr. Feld. Though he was a genius in business—his contracts are still used as examples in universities—and could spot trends long before the public knew what it wanted, everything he did was executed with passion. He had total commitment to every act or show he produced. Once he integrated us into his world and knew his production ran perfectly, he never lost his personal interest in us. He never ceased to invest time in our career.

Irvin flew from Washington twice a month to see the show. He came to the Frontier straight from the airport and sat in the elevated booth we had built for him as a birthday present, as if he were seeing us for the first time. He came backstage and did not just fill our egos with complimentary words but in the most diplomatic way suggested aspects of the show that could be improved upon.

You see, Irvin's other great gift was that he had a feel for people. He knew exactly how to give us criticism without our resenting it. He presented his comments in such a way that we were challenged.

After the first show, he didn't retire for the night, he watched the second performance, too, with the same enthusiasm, spontaneity, and joy.

At a certain point in the show, I always introduced him to the audience. And that was his moment. He beamed with pride and bowed to the audience as they applauded him.

Roy

After the second performance he went backstage and sprinkled his personal magic and enthusiasm on the cast, chatted with them, gave words of praise, and, believe it or not, acknowledged them one by one. And then he came to our private apartment at the

"He is great who is what he is from nature and who never reminds us of others."

Frontier, and with his Cognac and cigars, he sat with us and talked. He explored new ideas with us, proposed other ventures, and sometimes just shared stories and wisdom from his colorful life. Irvin was also Bernie's mentor, and so it was Bernie's ritual, around five A.M., to escort him to his room in the hotel. Irvin showered, changed his suit, and they went directly to the airport.

R*oy*

"He is great," Ralph Waldo Emerson said, "who is what he is from nature and who never reminds us of others." Irvin Feld was second to none; for us he soared as high as the eagle in the sky. When he died in 1984, for a moment all the lights and color went out of our life. But not for as long as it might have been. In a sense, he never left us. For Irvin's legacy—and his gift to us—was his son, Kenneth. It is often said that greatness skips a generation. The way the story usually plays out, the self-made man grooms a son to be

181

his successor, but the heir apparent can never live up to the achievement of the father; everything has been handed to him.

Siegfried

The most romantic ending to the Irvin Feld biography is that it worked entirely the opposite.

For there was one thing that Feld loved more than his empire: It was his family. And he nurtured them with the same passion and commitment.

Yes, Kenneth had a tremendous advantage, but it was a responsibility second to none to follow his father's path. He elected not to follow. Like his father, Kenneth is a man of his time, a visionary, with the ability to spot what the public wants, to take the empire—the circus, Walt Disney's *World on Ice*, which he conceived, and our show at the Mirage—and modernize it and globalize it.

In that respect he was groomed by his father. Irvin never wanted Kenneth to fill his shoes. He left him with the challenge to take the Feld organization to the next level. Is Kenneth his father's son? In the best sense of the word. He's completely and totally original, and like his father, he has, under incredible but different obstacles, made his own pair of shoes.

 # Kenneth Feld

Growing up in my father's business, I met every kind of performer, but I never met anyone like Siegfried and Roy. You couldn't categorize these two. Magicians, illusionists, animal specialists—the easy descriptions don't work at all. Siegfried and Roy are, first and foremost, performers. That means that their success depends not only on their ability to charm live audiences night after night, but also on the strength of their characters. You can't turn performers like this into stars, they have to be stars.

Siegfried and Roy would have been successful no matter what kind of entertainers they decided to be. If they had been able to sing, they might have been the world's biggest opera stars. If they had wanted to act, they would have been the world's biggest movie stars. Very seldom in a lifetime do you see people this gifted.

182

What makes them even more re-markable is that when they say their life is a stage, they're not just pro-moting something. The people you see onstage are the people you see at home. It's not an act, they're completely natural. From the moment they get up to the moment they go to sleep, they *are* Siegfried and Roy.

And that sincerity comes across to the public. It doesn't matter that Siegfried and Roy aren't absolutely articulate in English. What they communicate better than anyone is their love of the audience. As soon as they come onstage, people feel they know Siegfried and Roy—and they love them.

Kenneth Feld, the world's leading producer of live family entertainment and the producer of all our shows from television to stage since 1979

That's why I have such trouble describing what their shows are like. I could talk about the mechanical things, but that's not it. The power of their show is the heart and soul they put into it. For that, I tell people, you have to see them to understand them.

That's the special challenge of live performance. If you make a movie, twenty million people might see it in the first year; then it goes on television and on cassette, and hundreds of millions of people have an opportunity to experience it. There are no performers today, except Siegfried and Roy, who are pure live entertainers, capable of drawing seven hundred thousand people a year.

And yet, although they're based in Las Vegas, they're the most international performers in the world. That's the beauty of their show—they go beyond language, they're pure visual entertainment. When they went to Japan, it was terrific that they did the whole show in Japanese. But they didn't have to. They still would have grossed $55 million and been the highest-grossing performers of live entertainment in Japan's history.

With an attitude like that, it's not surprising that Siegfried and Roy's career is one long upward growth curve. They've never been on the wane, never hit a dip. They'll continue to grow because they're constantly improving and perfecting their show, and because they give 110 percent each night.

It's a pleasure working with them because they breed such loyalty. I remember the first TV show we did together, a 1977 special featuring Günther Gebel-Williams. My father and I had the right to edit Siegfried and Roy's segment, a fact of major concern to them. But the day after the show, they sent us a telegram: "This is the greatest thing we've ever seen, you did a wonderful job, thank you." That's unheard of, performers just don't do that. This gesture was important for them—it was the first time someone had delivered exactly what had been promised. And what came out of that was trust.

Bernie Yuman is undyingly loyal to them, and they to him; he delivered, and they trusted him as well. That's the wonderful thing about working with Siegfried and Roy; they have a real sense for people and a great ability to behave appropriately. I see that clearly in my own relationship with them. I can never be what my father was to them. After he died, I worked like crazy to establish my own imprint on the business. It was a time of testing, and I know there were many who weren't sure that I was up to it. The only ones who were in my corner from day one were Siegfried and Roy. In that, they're very much like my father—they take people and bring them to new heights by their presence and their personality. They expect the best of people; in order not to disappoint them, you find you've surpassed yourself. It's not just the audience that gets pumped up around Siegfried and Roy.

Roy

Like the Ringling Brothers and Barnum & Bailey Circus, we are now a part of the Feld heritage. In the seven years since his father's death, Kenneth has been a driving force in our progression from the Frontier to our Japanese world tour to Radio City Music Hall and to the Mirage. We are proud to say he is not only our producer but, more important, our friend.

Siegfried

One hour and forty minutes all to ourselves.

What to do?

The first time ever in the history of Las Vegas that two magicians, or even a single magician, ever had their own show. It was certainly the most original challenge we'd ever faced. For now we were more than just illusionists; we were, in the true sense of the word, "entertainers." The word on the Strip was that we were destined to fall flat on our faces. Who wanted to watch nearly two hours of magic?

People didn't understand that we had a unique advantage.

As foreigners we had come to this strange place fresh and unjaded. We had developed our act without preconceptions. And because we were never fully comfortable with the prescribed Las Vegas formulas, we were able to look at the phenomenon of Las Vegas with a detached eye.

As we saw it, Las Vegas was on the verge of a complete personality change. When we arrived in 1970, Vegas was a gambler's town, pure and simple. By 1981 it was becoming something else: a destination, a resort. The creation of the Convention Center had a lot to do with that; it lured younger and more international visitors to Vegas. That audience was ready for something different. This was the audience of the future.

The impresarios of the ongoing Vegas shows were not rushing to provide that. But that was understandable; for years they had underestimated the Vegas audience.

It's a show business truism that New York is the toughest audience. While New York may have a more sophisticated audience, it's also a more unified one. When we played Radio City Music Hall in 1989, for instance, it was a lark to perform there; the people were focused.

For me, the Las Vegas audience is more of a challenge. Here they are, tourists of every nationality, visiting a place that was built for pleasure, intent on escaping reality. Yet they can't simply sit back and enjoy the show. Just the opposite. They're distracted at every turn. They enter the theater having just lost a bundle, with their minds still back at the gambling table or slot machine. Or they've just flown thousands of miles and have jet lag. Or they've just been married. Or divorced. And swirling around them are waiters taking orders and serving drinks. Small wonder that casino owners regarded their long-term shows as nothing more than a rest period between gambling sessions. Bring on the scantily clad show girls, strike up the band, tell some jokes, and you've got a show.

With such low expectations, Las Vegas entertainment became stagnant. As a rule, the shows didn't make money. They didn't have to; they were just "something to do." The hotel owners knew that the money they lost in the theater would come back to them tenfold in the casino. The customers accepted second-class entertainment—glitzy, ooh-la-la nude revues—because "That's Vegas." So there was no incentive from any direction to improve the quality of the shows.

oy

Why change? Because it was all we knew how to do. And because every time we changed our show, the audience responded.

Over the years our fans wrote us, not asking how we vanished the elephant or the tiger but thanking us for the experience. Clearly they were getting a message that we hadn't yet made explicit. That encouraged us, for we wanted to break down more of the barriers. We wanted to do more than just sell a series of magic effects.

Idealism has its limitations, particularly in Vegas. We took what we had done at the Stardust and in our television shows and put it in different wrappings. And we came up with a theme—the ongoing battle between good and evil—and developed a story line around the illusions that drew on myths and fables.

Unlike our show at the Mirage, which is a fully integrated presentation, we still had to go with the flow of Las Vegas to a certain degree at the Frontier. *Beyond Belief* was halfway between the old days—a series of illusions separated by unrelated production numbers that featured bare-breasted show girls in sequins and feathers—and what we do today.

Though we followed the formula of having specialty acts in between our production, we wanted something fresh and modern. Because the Felds owned the circus, we had the opportunity to choose from one of their many acts. We chose the King Charles Troupe, a black basketball team that played the game on unicycles. Irvin and Kenneth had discovered them in the Bronx; they were all poor street kids, and their act still had a raw edge to it. Pretty soon we had the troupe break dancing and, even as early as 1981, singing rap.

For Vegas this act was a total novelty. We incorporated all of the men into our finale production, and they led a white show girl down a huge staircase. This was met with extreme disapproval by the hotel bosses. Until this time there was a limited number of black show dancers, and never before had black dancers actually accompanied a white dancer. We were told we simply could not do this in Vegas.

For us the King Charles Troupe was more than just a transitional act; we felt they gave our show more body and created an interesting contrast with what we were doing. We had music written especially for the troupe and gave them special lighting. The audience was crazy for the King Charles Troupe and would rock out of their chairs to the rhythm of the music.

Neva—gambling's official mascot and the Nevada Gaming Commission's official photo

A modern history of
levitation as performed
by Siegfried and Roy

Ever since he was a child, the maharaja of Rewa had been fascinated by the tiger inscribed on his family's coat of arms. It was a strain of tiger that no other country in the world supposedly had, one that the maharaja had only heard of and never seen. With charcoal gray or chocolate brown stripes on a coat of white fur, this phantom species—believed in India to be a reincarnation of the messengers of the gods—is known as the white tiger. And it was elusive indeed. Through the years the maharaja had hunted the jungle, hoping to capture one.

Did it really exist? History had it that over the last fifty years hunters had spotted nine of these tigers in the jungles of Orissa, Madhya Pradesh, and Assam, but their existence was only ascertained when, in 1951, in the forests of Rewa, the maharaja found a white cub.

The maharaja took his dream tiger back to his palace and christened him Mohan. In Mohan, he thought he had found his destiny: to breed his white tiger and restore the species. He was mated with a normal striped tigress, and the maharaja could only hope that Mohan carried the genes necessary to produce a litter of white cubs. Of course, if it had been that simple, I might not be telling this story.

Seven years and many litters of golden cubs later, the maharaja was about to give up when, by accident, Mohan mated with one of his offspring. In 1958 she produced one male and three female white cubs. The maharaja had found the key: All the golden offspring were heterozygous, carriers of the white gene. He could take all his gold tigers and mate them back to white ones. As a result of this discovery, more white tiger cubs soon followed.

To the outside world, these captive white tigers were the only ones in existence. To the maharaja they were his jewels of nature and proud possessions; they were part of his family. Eventually he turned his summer palace on the lake at Govindgarh into a domain for his tigers, and they freely roamed all 120 rooms and palace gardens.

Though he was possessive of these crown jewels of nature, he didn't lose sight of his ultimate goal. Before he died, he bequeathed one white offspring to the New Delhi Zoo and another to the National Zoo in Washington, D.C. From there, a loan was made to the Cincinnati Zoo, which successfully produced a perfect breeding pair. It was this pair in Cincinnati that became the foundation for the perpetuation of the white tiger. Along with his bequests the maharaja made the stipulation that prohibited the zoos from ever selling a white tiger to a private individual. It was his wish for the public to enjoy them.

When the maharaja of Baroda finished telling how the mythological saga of the white tiger of India—my dream—was a reality, I was at a loss for words. I had heard of white

The Maharajah of Rewa's family coat of arms had a golden tiger and a white tiger.
After many years of dreaming and searching for the elusive white tiger, in 1951 he found one in
the jungles of Rewa. As a tribute to the Maharajah and as heirs to the perpetuation of the
white tiger, we adapted his coat of arms.

tigers, I knew they were extinct in the wild, but I had no idea there were any in captivity. At that moment, all I wanted was for the maharaja to get me an introduction to the Cincinnati Zoo so I could see the tigers and possibly become involved in protecting them against extinction. This, of course, would be difficult to achieve because of the deceased maharaja's requirements.

The maharaja of Baroda felt that because of our sincere love and respect for our animals, my philosophy of affection training, and the success we'd had with raising animals to live in our environment, if any private individuals could carry out the dreams of the maharaja of Rewa, it was us.

After many long months of artful negotiation by the maharaja of Baroda and meetings with Edward J. Maruska, the chairman of the Zoological Society of Cincinnati, we made a personal and financial commitment to aid in the preservation of the white tiger. In effect, we became a part of the zoo's breeding team.

It was agreed that we would choose a male and a female from the next litter born. We waited anxiously to hear that two of the females were pregnant. Later, after what seemed like ages, we got the long-awaited telephone call that both had given birth. The zoo

Royal encounter
*The maharajah of Baroda, who is the commissioner of Indian wildlife, has a first meeting
with Sitarra, our snow-white tiger and the matriarch of the Royal White Tigers of Nevada.
For the Maharajah, a snow-white species had only been a phantom tiger that appeared
in Indian mythology.*

offered to make the choice for me. But I was too excited. I had to go to Cincinnati and
see all the cubs for myself. After the second evening's performance, Bernie and I boarded
a red-eye flight to Cincinnati.

The instant I entered the nursery, my eyes locked with only one—a snow white baby
without any stripes at all.

There, before me, was my white dream tiger.

For the experts at the Cincinnati Zoo, this pure white cub was indeed a phenomenon
of nature, but the zoo already had two adult snow white females, and neither had ever
given birth. They assumed this rarity was sterile.

The moment I saw the cub I suddenly felt as if I had some higher purpose in life, that
my destiny lay in this tiny snowball of a creature.

Neva

Sitarra

Shasadee

Was the snow white tiger ever a species, or is it a freak of nature? We don't know. A sighting of one in the wild has never been recorded. My own theory is that it did exist, but being pure white, it could not camouflage itself in the forest from its predators. And because of that, it seems only natural to me that white tigers became extinct long before any other tigers.

I chose my two white tiger cubs, one from each litter, which would be the breeding pair: a male called Neva, which is short for Nevada and means "snow" in Spanish, and Shasadee, the female, which means "the chosen one."

But what I wanted more than anything in life was the snow white cub. I was determined to take her home with me. Because she was considered of no value to the breeding program, the board of directors at the zoo didn't really understand my interest and fascination. And at this crucial moment I wasn't going to tell them of my wild dream and have them think their new sponsor was just a bit nuts. There was no opposition from them to let me take her home with me.

With my sense of destiny set in motion, I made a stipulation that if ever a snow white *male* was born either at the zoo or within our joint breeding program, I would be allowed to have it.

I named my dream tiger Sitarra, which means "star of India." For me, she was more than just a phenomenon of nature. I had total belief from the moment I laid eyes on her that she would mate and have babies. Besides the commitment and dedication to preserving the white tiger, I had a larger, more personal dream: to bring back or create—whichever you believe—the snow white tiger species.

Siegfried

And me, the conjurer, what did I do? I sat back and watched the magic.

We can speculate that it was just sheer coincidence that Sitarra gave birth. We'll never know, but I believe that Roy's spiritual connection to her had something to do with it. He meditated with her from the time she was a cub. Occasionally I spied on them through the crack of the door. Roy sat in his meditation position, with Sitarra sitting next to him. As Roy's whole being moved to another plane of consciousness, Sitarra seemed to go there, too. They were so in tune with each other that when Roy's head nodded, Sitarra's instantly followed. And when, at the end of a session, Roy snapped awake, so did Sitarra.

And then there was Roy's vision of the habitat he wanted to build for the white tigers. I always envisioned something Bavarian: green and rocky, basically traditional surroundings, with trees and little streams. But Roy—well, he creates his own world, and you can only assume it's not going to be like anyone else's.

"I know exactly what it should be," he told me one morning over breakfast. "I'd like to give the tigers an environment in which everything is snow white."

I couldn't believe what I was hearing. I was furious. No way, in my backyard, was that going to happen. We had endless fights over this.

Roy

It was just something my instinct told me. The maharaja of Baroda told me that three hundred years ago the original home of the white tiger had been the foothills of the Himalayas. So the scenery around them was snow-covered mountains. This is mere speculation, but perhaps these snow-covered hills had been a source of camouflage. As they moved farther away, they lost this protection. I wanted to give them a feeling of the security of their original environment.

Siegfried

There was something we both noticed about the white tigers. When they were with Roy or onstage with us, they were calm and secure. At the time our facilities for the animals

The royal white tiger habitat

Our home for this endangered species is the best of both worlds—green lawns and palm trees, gushing waterfalls, but the predominant feature is that it is all white, to remind them of their ancestors' home when they were camouflaged at the foothills of the snow-covered Himalayas.

197

were very uniform; each had an enclosed space, but they were side by side. When the white tigers were in this space, they seemed unsettled. I finally came around to thinking that perhaps they did need a unique environment. So I gave in to what Roy envisioned.

I still had my doubts as I watched the structure being built. It seemed cold and uninviting. Though it had mirrorlike pools and gushing waterfalls, I still couldn't understand how any creature could feel secure in such glacial surroundings. But the moment the white tigers entered the habitat I knew Roy was right. A tranquillity that I hadn't seen before came over them. And the real proof that they were happy was that three days after the new habitat was completed the romance between Neva and Sitarra began to flourish and they mated.

And it happened right before our very eyes.

This was in 1986, and until now Shasadee—our chosen one—and Neva had mated, but she hadn't conceived. Though we had what was called a perfect breeding pair, the perfect male still has to accept the female that's been selected for him. It's fairly simple. Like human attraction, their sexual sparks have to be there. Shasadee just never excited him. She was too docile and passive for him. It was Sitarra who really excited Neva, and to this day he has never shown the same interest in any other female. And it's the same for her.

Their torrid Romeo and Juliet love affair has since produced four more litters. The first time I saw them mating it was unreal to watch, for it's more like a fight than a love scene. So rough, in fact, that Siegfried and I thought they were trying to kill each other. Or rather I thought Sitarra was going to kill Neva. The moment Neva penetrated her, her ice blue eyes seemed to ooze hot, piercing blue fire, her hissing so deep, so sharp, the sound alone could cut you in half, and then she went after him and beat him. To our surprise, Neva just stood there and took it like a man. Another male would have fought back. Obviously this was Neva's way of handling her. And though it was frightening, it convinced me more than ever that Sitarra would conceive.

Of course, no one believed me.

After Neva and Sitarra's passionate recognition scene—twenty-eight times in two hours—I kept telling everyone she was pregnant. We had no way of knowing, but she seemed larger to me. One day, after I'd been repeating my prediction for a couple of

The magic of nature
Sitarra changes the tide of history by becoming the first snow-white tiger to give birth in captivity.

months, I was meditating with Sitarra, and I was positive I felt little ones kicking. Still neither Siegfried nor our veterinarian and zoological experts believed me. Siegfried was now calling it Sitarra's permanent pregnancy.

I was so positive that I wouldn't allow Sitarra to perform in the death-defying crystal chamber, as she had been doing every night. I still brought her to the theater with me, and one evening, after meditating with her, I noticed a little blood where she had been resting.

I was certain this would be the night of the blessed event. After the second show I took Sitarra home immediately and made her comfortable in the nursery we had built for future arrivals. I settled in with her, and she rested with her head in my arms. Sometime around four in the morning Sitarra went into labor.

Her first little one came out encased in its sac. She artfully cleaned the baby, bit the cord with her teeth, picked the newborn up with her mouth, carried it over to me, and placed it in my lap for safekeeping. She then lay down beside me to rest again and wait.

The moment was so special, so completely tender, I didn't want to break the feeling, but I was also worried. I had to wake someone up in the house. We needed to get the vet right away in case there was a complication. I stood and made my way to the exit door. At that moment Sitarra sensed I was going to leave, so she picked up the baby, dangled it between her huge fangs, went to the door, and blocked it. I had no choice but to stay.

Fortunately, just after she had the first baby, the rest of our animals, from the lions to the leopards, started to roar, heralding the arrival. They instinctively knew something had happened. Their concert of howls woke everyone up in the house. Even the birds sleeping in the trees awoke and, with their chittering and chattering, added to the cacophony. At this point Toney came outside and peeked into the den. He was soon joined by Siegfried and Lynette. I held one finger up to let them know how many babies Sitarra had so far.

Sitarra gave birth to three white cubs: SiegRoy, Vegas, and Nevada. It was the first time ever in captivity that a snow white female had given birth.

Siegfried

I stood silently outside the door so as not to disturb them. It was something quite unbelievable. Sitarra's head was resting on Roy in total exhaustion; the cub was in his

Sitarra and her first litter—SiegRoy, Vegas, and Nevada—meet the press. As you can see by her ferocious expression, Sitarra was in complete control of the inaugural photo session.

Sitarra
*Our goddess of the white-tiger world and procreator of the Siegfried and Roy
Royal White Tigers of Nevada*

lap. The silence so acute you could hear it. Then the next baby started to come. And the third. With each birth she again cleaned the cub and gave it to Roy.

All the words in the world cannot describe this moment: the way Sitarra included Roy in the birth almost as if he were the father, the cries of her pain with each delivery and her face changing from a girl to mother, and, after it was over, the look of serenity in her eyes. To have the privilege to see this was to witness a miracle—a holy moment. I'd never felt so close to God and nature. I now knew that there really was someone up above.

Roy

As magicians, how could we top this? This was the greatest magic we'd ever witnessed. We knew the time would come when we would want to put the cubs in the show. But how could we do it so the audience could experience it through our eyes? How could we get this magical moment across to our audience?

The event put us on a different plane; it unlocked the key to so many thoughts and feelings we wanted to share with the audience, but until now we hadn't been able to put it in a context. We could disappear, reappear, fly, and float—realize just about any fantasy we wanted—but Sitarra's giving birth was beyond anything we could ever do.

The purity of the moment had humbled us. We wanted to present these gems of nature without illusion or stage effects. We wanted simply to pay homage to the magic and miracle of life and nature.

After Sitarra gave birth, we decided to give a name to the breeding line that we were establishing. We christened them the Royal White Tigers of Nevada. It bothered me that a state as beautiful as Nevada always seemed to be synonymous with gambling, quickie divorce, and the Mustang Ranch. Naming the cubs after Nevada was our way of giving something back to the city, state, and community that had given us so much opportunity to flourish. As the fastest-growing city in America, it's inevitable that Las Vegas will take on a more cultural face. We have our own ballet company. The University of Nevada at Las Vegas, which has long had one of the best college basketball teams in the country, the Rebels, is also becoming known as an academic institution. It is my hope that to the state's future generation, the Royal White Tigers will be synonymous with Nevada.

As Sitarra's cubs got a bit bigger, I began to raise them in the same way I've raised all

Red, White, and Blue
—born on July 4, 1989, in Japan—look on as Roy shares a tender
moment with their mother, Sitarra.

Family ski trip
A major dilemma! High up on the slopes of Mt. Charleston with six sets of
legs and only two pairs of skis

my animals, by incorporating them into our surroundings at home, taking them to the theater at night in their little basket, and then, when they're old enough, putting them in the show.

Like a proud parent, I photograph or film every first moment in my animal's growth. Sitarra's first afternoon out on the lawn with her cubs roaming and exploring their surroundings was documented on film. It was when Siegfried and I looked at the footage that we figured out how to present the babies to the audience. We would give them a glimpse of the magic that we have the privilege of seeing every day of our lives. We would just show the film.

Siegfried

Everyone at the Frontier looked at us as if we had really flipped this time. In the middle of a show on the Strip we were going to pull out a film of tigers running around on the lawn? First the covered show girls, then this. Would we next announce that we had converted to the Mormon faith and were moving our show to Salt Lake City?

Sitarra's giving birth was a turning point. For so long I'd wanted to find a way to establish some sort of intimacy with my audience. The time had come to show something of ourselves. You can't preach; you can't tell; you have to *show* them. A good entertainer is one who has the talent to work with all the emotions and stir them up in his audience. I felt I needed to get underneath the skin of my audience and make more emotional contact. I couldn't see adding more illusions. If anything, I wanted to give the audience some time to catch their breaths. We were taking a risk with the film because the transition could bring the energy level way down. We were asking our audience to switch gears: to go from swashbuckling, lightning-speed fantasy to sensitivity and to see the experience of man and nature in total harmony. A lot to ask for.

It would work only if the transition were made with a grand ending, which is how the idea evolved to drive Sitarra and her cubs onstage in a vintage Rolls-Royce. Muhammad Ali, who's been a close, personal friend of Bernie Yuman's for thirty years, knew of a 1930s Rolls in mint condition that belonged to Greta Garbo. Muhammad managed to make all the necessary connections to approach Miss Garbo, who, in a gesture that seemed out of character, gave it to us. At the Frontier Sitarra got out of the white Rolls and walked over to a white rock formation that was surrounded by white palm trees, the

Clash of the Titans

essence of purity. She lay on top of it and all her babies came to her. It was a touching, adorable moment, and we got the right response: It raised the audience's energy level again.

Roy

We also felt the film deserved a piece of music especially written for it. With one line, "Bless the beast and bless the children," Siegfried and I went to our composer and musical director, Jerry Bilik, and asked if he could write something around that refrain.

Neither of us is musical, and it was hard for Jerry to interpret what we wanted. In our heads we heard something soulful, spiritual, something with a touch of gospel, almost like "Old Man River." Jerry hired a group of black studio singers. We went to the recording studio to listen to them mix the tape. It still wasn't the right feel. So we singled out the lead singer, showed him the film, and asked him to sing the song, not the way he was directed but through his heart. Out came this beautiful, resonant voice with all the emotion that we felt.

The song would accompany not only the film but also the moment when I went up on the floating mirror ball. In the middle of conceiving the film and song, however, my dear beloved Sahra had started to fail, and she was no longer able to float up with me. I decided to put Neva in the illusion. The first night Neva performed it, we introduced the new song—"Bless the Beasts and Bless the Children"—and it was that night that I bade my beloved Sahra her farewell. It was the end and the beginning.

I guess you could say that as the babies grew, we grew with the responsibility. Our work on and sponsorship of the breeding and preservation of the white tiger gave us in a sense another career and commitment. Through the film we were able to share with the audience what has become, along with being entertainers, a total extension of ourselves. Today we are honorary chairmen of the Zoological Society of Cincinnati. The white tiger is rarer than the panda bear, which still exists in the wild. There are fewer than two hundred white tigers in existence. Fortunately through our efforts the numbers are increasing, and there is now hope that this species will survive the turn of the century. Our ultimate goal—and one that won't be achieved in our lifetime—is to be able to release the white tiger back into the wild, in an environment where it will be able to roam freely and safely.

Our white tiger family has grown to a total of twenty-three, and we now have five snow whites. Less than a year after Sitarra gave birth, another miracle happened. Akbar Kabul, the first-ever snow white male, was born. Another male—Mantra—was born in 1990.

Right now we're paving the way for the possibility of a third wonder. If two snow white tigers can mate and create a snow white cub, nature has given us a second chance.

Nineteen eighty-seven. An eventful year. *Beyond Belief* was in its sixth year. The show had not lost its sparkle or drawing power. We were still playing two sold-out performances every night, but the problem for us was that we were still turning away as many as three thousand people a day, even though the hotel had broken through the walls and extended the theater out into the casino. There was no more room. We knew it was time for us to move on.

To put it bluntly, we knew we were the single hottest attraction in Las Vegas, and we knew we now had the power to have a show that would be a total break from the Las Vegas mold of entertainment. What we wanted was to be in business with someone who shared our vision. And there was only one man who understood the relentless staleness of the Strip. As it turned out, he was ready to smash all the formulas to create something modern, which, for Las Vegas, meant different.

Steve Wynn was, long before 1987, the golden boy of the casino industry. In 1973, when he was only thirty-one, he took over the Golden Nugget, a seedy and failing casino in downtown Las Vegas, and turned it into a classy, glittering, high-profile money machine. In the late seventies he opened another in the just-developed Atlantic City. Mr. Wynn was a natural showman who wrote his television ads and took equal billing with stars like Frank Sinatra and Dolly Parton in the commercials.

Now he was embarked on the most ambitious project in the history of Las Vegas: On the last undeveloped lot on the Strip, he would erect the most extraordinary hotel-casino ever built. His vision was so far beyond what anyone had ever done in Vegas that if you wanted to compare him to anyone, you'd have to say he was like Walt Disney. Except in his fantasy, there was no kiddie park. What Steve Wynn wanted was to give his clientele class and style on a grand scale. There would be no neon signs or sequins and bare-breasted shows.

Mr. Wynn showed us the model of his dream hotel—appropriately named the Mirage—which was scheduled to open in 1989. It was so much an extension of our imagination. He wanted to create an exotic jungle atmosphere—a blend of Caribbean and Far Eastern—with rain forests and erupting volcanoes. For years Siegfried and I had toyed with the idea of creating our own hotel that would be rich in wild fantasy, something that was an extension of our environment. Steve Wynn's idea was the closest to our dream than anything we'd ever heard. The idea was a natural for us.

Steve Wynn

When I was developing the concept for the hotel, Siegfried and Roy fit into my visions very early on. In Las Vegas the most difficult and the most elusive decision is entertainment. To sustain an entertainment policy with any relativity to cost is nearly impossible. Las Vegas showrooms have been losing three to five million dollars a year for many years, and I'm speaking of shows that featured big stars.

Revues like the Folies-Bergère at the Tropicana or the Stardust/Lido lost less per show because of their reliance upon production rather than famous stars. But these spectaculars had long ago begun to get stale in concept. Topless women marching up and down a staircase should have gone out in the fifties; that was an antiquated idea imported from France after the Second World War. In Europe that kind of show was done with taste and flair; in Las Vegas it was just T&A.

As for the stars, this town used to be the most wonderful place to work. Prior to 1970 a live cabaret entertainer reached the peak by working in Las Vegas; it was the most important place to play, and the biggest salaries were earned here. You could earn fifty to seventy thousand dollars a week for fourteen shows.

With the advent of rock acts in the early seventies, the phenomenon of the one-night concert tour arose. And with it came a fundamental change in the entertainment business. It started with the rock stars, but it took over and included all kinds of entertainers; even Frank Sinatra started doing one-nighters. Entertainers could now go to a city, play to five, ten, or even twenty thousand people for two hours, and earn up to two hundred thousand dollars for the evening.

The magic of
Steve Wynn and
Siegfried and Roy
at "our" Mirage

As a result of playing a big venue, the performers had to magnify their show with lots of lighting effects and massive speakers. Everything had to be as good as a record; intimacy was out. Las Vegas became yesterday's news. It no longer made sense for someone like Kenny Rogers to play Vegas and get six hundred thousand dollars for twelve shows when he could go on the road and make a million and a half for the same number. For a major star to do two shows a night of the magnitude necessary for the big halls was not only too tough physically but certain to lose money; the hotels just couldn't afford it.

That's why the entertainment for the Mirage was the most complex issue for me. How could I get people to come? Glamour and celebrity are still essential to the Las Vegas

Frolicking in the snow during a photo shoot for Bognor's new line of Siegfried and Roy skiwear

experience; although prices had changed, the need for show entertainment had not.

For me there was only one sure bet: the biggest act in the history of Las Vegas—Siegfried and Roy. At the Frontier they had done capacity business, twice a night, forty-four weeks a year, for *seven years*! There is no major star I could have put in that showroom; the crowds would not have come. Any other entertainer would have burned out, but Siegfried and Roy were wrapped in their magic and a production show. With them I knew I had the best of both worlds: the sustaining value of the production and the marquee value of their magic.

Beyond all that, I also wanted to find talent that would be as unique as everything else

With our friend Willy Bogner, the chairman and owner of Bogner Skiwear, who created the Siegfried and Roy Royal White Tiger line of ski clothing

To strengthen the blood line of the white tiger we mated one with a golden tiger and produced our first litter of gold heterosygus tigers—carriers of the white gene. If mated back to a white species, they will produce a new generation of Siegfried and Roy white tigers.

Moments Later

After giving birth to three cubs, Noel was too exhausted to tend to her fourth arrival, and that is the most crucial moment.

There is one thing you should never do—go near a tigress when she's giving birth. She's fully capable of killing you, her mate, or her cub. But I'm ruled by my instinct and heart. At that moment, it didn't occur to me I was risking my life. All I could see was a helpless cub and I knew if I didn't enter the habitat and help, it would suffocate. I slowly crawled toward Noel, speaking softly to her as I reached between her hind legs. I picked up the little one, broke the umbilical cord with my thumbs, opened the birth sac, removed the mucus from the baby's face and mouth to prevent suffocation, and crawled back to Noel.

At first, she was too weary to notice, but then she looked up and watched my every move. I placed the wet newborn between her front paws. She regained her strength and took charge. I wasn't sure if the cub was alive, but a few seconds later a tiny cry of life came forth. Amen.

Easter 1992
Five months later, four happy and healthy gold heterosygus cubs

Gildah on the Lake

*To give a five-ton elephant the pleasure of a swimming party on Las Vegas's beautiful
Lake Mead is no easy feat. But to feed hundreds of underprivileged children ice cream in
115-degree heat was a magical attempt. We succeeded.
Bravo, Gildah, bravo!*

I was creating for the Mirage. I wanted an act that would be a continuation of the hotel's
fantasy quality. And that, too, pointed an arrow directly to Siegfried and Roy.

R*oy*

Mr. Wynn's offer was dazzling. He not only would build a theater to our specifications
and create a replica of our own white tiger habitat but would give us carte blanche to
do the kind of show we wanted without any interferences. And he would give us an
unprecedented contract in the history of live entertainment: a $57.5 million guarantee
for five years. What could we say to that? Only this: We would report to work in the
winter of 1990.

S*iegfried*

We talk about our show, we talk about our contracts, we talk about the people we work
with, but the fact is we also have a life. After more than twenty years in Las Vegas we're

definitely natives and active members of the community. But although we've always identified more with the American spirit and way of life—we're American citizens—people who've never met us would be surprised to discover how German we really are. We've never dismissed our roots.

In a way we've transported as much of Germany as possible to Las Vegas. On eighty acres in the middle of the desert, we've built a Bavarian cottage and created a landscape that is a reminder of my Bavarian upbringing—lush green grass, thousands of trees, streams and bridges and picturesque ponds filled with ducks, black swans, and King Ludwigs. We also have horses, goats, and chickens, and dozens of white peacocks roam the grassy meadows. Close the gates, and you're in southern Germany. At home we still eat our hearty German cooking, and as much as possible we try to incorporate some of the customs of German homelife into ours.

Seconds after this photo was taken, Sleeping Beauty's Castle vanished at the hands of Siegfried and Roy.

When we appeared in the "Magic in the Magic Kingdom" TV Special in 1988, in addition
to making Disneyland's Sleeping Beauty Castle disappear, we also decided to transform a
five-ton elephant into George Burns. Our big worry was that George wasn't agile enough
for this rapid-speed effect. "Don't worry, I run twice around the block every day to stay fit,"
George reassured us.

Well, more than several takes later we finally had a winner. Whoof, puff, explosion, the
elephant vanished and George appeared right beside Roy. George, however, forgot to say his lines:
"Beware, in the next few moments, my friends, Siegfried and Roy will attempt to make the
Sleeping Beauty Castle disappear." Instead he turned to Roy, who, in a warm gesture had
instinctively put his arm around the veteran pocket dynamo, and said,
"Gee, kid, it hasn't felt this good in anybody's arms since Gracie."
Thanks, George, I took it as a compliment.

217

With Roy's mother, Johanna Horn

R*oy*

Years ago, when it was clear that Nevada was going to be my permanent home, I invited my mother to leave Germany and live in a house I would build for her. In the early days she looked after Siegfried and me and became the good spirit of the house. She is today a symbol of continuity, a connection to my roots. Remembering what she went through during my childhood, I resolved to try to make the rest of her life as secure and untroubled as possible. It gives me immense pleasure to be reminded daily that I was able to do this for her. And she takes pleasure in making sure her son has a "good German home."

S*iegfried*

We make a yearly visit back to the old country. We still get homesick. We miss the atmosphere, the smell of a certain coffeehouse, a certain restaurant. It's not so much a

German way of life as that hit of European atmosphere that we need to replenish our spirits.

Except for a television special we did in June 1991 for German television we haven't performed in Germany in twenty-five years, yet we're considered two of its most famous exports. It was the greatest feeling when we were there to do the special to have people come up to us for autographs and pull out Mirage ticket stubs.

We've been awarded the Iron Cross and Order of Merit, the country's highest honor, which is usually reserved for diplomats and dignitaries. On that day two German boys who had embarked on a career that was considered a Gypsy's profession had to ask themselves, "Really? For *us*?"

A rare holiday together

Unlike most teams in the entertainment business, Siegfried and I grow stronger.
But working together for three decades . . . we need to get away from one another.
When we have a vacation, we flee in opposite directions. This was the rare time
when we found ourselves together in Acapulco.
Good thing! Otherwise I wouldn't be here to tell our story.
One afternoon we went swimming at a beautiful beach. I swam out too far,
then I realized the current was so strong that I couldn't get back. I noticed that Siegfried was
swimming out too far, so I sent him panicked hand signals.
By now, I had little strength or breath left. The current pulled me under and I began taking
in water. Suddenly, I felt something grab me by the hair, hold me underneath the arm and
pull me back to the beach. My chest was pumped, I spit out a lot of water,
I looked up, and it was Siegfried.
Instead of fighting the current, he had drifted out on an angle, caught up with me, and dragged
me to shore. He saved my life—and he's never let me forget it.

220

Receiving the Iron Cross and Order of Merit
*Germany's highest award—the ceremony took place
in Las Vegas at the Jungle Palace. It couldn't have
happened to two nicer guys.*

Blind and deaf children visiting the Jungle Palace

*How to tell them about the animals? "Show them through your eyes," their teacher
told Siegfried and me. So we pretended they were just like regular children.
But like the Pied Piper, we made everything bigger and more colorful.*

"May I touch a tiger?" a little blind girl asked.

*Siegfried and I knelt with her beside our golden tiger Sahra and we placed the child's
hand on her fur.*

"Where are the stripes?" she asked.

*"This is a black stripe and this a gold one . . ." And carefully, stripe by stripe,
we guided her hand across Sahra's back.*

*The joy in this child's face is something I'll never forget. And there was no question
in our minds—that little girl saw that tiger.*

June 1991: With Phantasialand owners, Sohni Löffelhardt (left) and Richard Schmidt (right), and the Bee Gees, during the taping of the German television special celebrating the twenty-fifth anniversary of Phantasialand

Pandemonium and a big reception greet us as we arrive in Germany for the TV special—our first performance there in twenty-five years.

Celebrating with German super-model Claudia Schiffer at the Bambi Awards

Receiving the Bambi Award
When we went to Germany to accept the country's most prestigious media award for our TV special, everyone was disappointed we didn't bring one of our white tigers. When we heard of their disappointment, we had an idea—why not make the symbolic Bambi trophy come alive?
That's us—great with animals!

The magic of her heart matches the magic of her beauty.
Joining together with Audrey Hepburn to receive our Bambi Awards

Roy riding in the desert with his Lippizaner stallion, Grandissimo

I protect my animals, they protect me. Once while riding with Grandissimo in the foothills of Mt. Charleston, I discovered a narrow mountain trail. After a long trip up this tricky path, there was a plateau with a stream, a few trees, rocks, and lots of thorn bushes. The sun was beating down, so I decided to give us both a rest. I unsaddled Grandissimo, who went to drink happily out of the stream. For myself, I spotted a sunny spot on a flat rock and, using the saddle as a pillow, I thought I'd take a rest.

Just as I settled in, I first heard and then saw a rattlesnake. My impulse was to move away, but when I did, I tripped and fell backward; in an instant, the snake was next to my legs, ready to strike. At the same time, Grandissimo—who had followed me to the rock—shrieked at the highest pitch and like lightning reared up. His hooves came crashing down on the snake, over and over. Foaming at the mouth, his large black eyes still flashing and blowing air through his nostrils, he came over to me and nudged and nuzzled me with his head.

Now, I ask you—is that friendship?

Roy

A great portion of my private life is devoted
to my animals. When I listen to people talk
about their children, I'm always amazed at
how similar their experiences are to mine.
For the relationship I have with my animals
is very much like that of a parent and child.
The one you love the most is often the
one that gives you the most trouble; the
troubled one always gets the most attention. Sound familiar?

As the father figure to my animals I love
the rewards I reap from nurturing them. All
the time, love, and effort I put into an
animal come back to me tenfold. It is, of
course, easier to get that result when I raise
an animal from a cub; he's immediately
conditioned to the environment.

It's much more difficult to create a loving
and affectionate animal when I adopt a fully
grown one. Then I have to undo fears, inse-
curities, and mistrusts that have developed
in his past. You could say in this situation
I'm not only a parent but also a psychiatrist.

Author, Roy, at work
*After a literary dispute, I transformed our writer,
Annette Tapert, into another creature in hope
that she could get deeper into my thoughts.*

People often ask me to describe my relationship with my animals. I've discovered the
only way I can is through specific stories. Take, for example, Macumba.

One day I got a call from my veterinarian, Marty Dinnes, with a plea to give a
magnificent black panther a home. His owner, who had died of a heart attack, had raised
him on a poor run-down ranch in California. Days after his death the ranch hands realized
they now had to deal with an unruly and heartbroken panther that had never had contact
with anyone except his master. Totally withdrawn in his sorrow, Macumba refused to
eat and resented anyone who tried to approach him; the handlers had no choice but to
cage him. And because a placement in a zoo couldn't be arranged, it was only a matter
of time before this beautiful specimen would be put down.

An encounter with Macuma

"I told you not to wear that hat."
*"Yes, and I told you not to tell me what to do all the
time," says Roy to Manchu—a very bossy snow
leopard.*

Marty's last stab at an attempt to save him was me. The story sounded similar to that of Jahmal, the unruly jaguar, so I had my doubts, but because I'm a sucker for the underdog, Macumba came home with me. During the next few weeks, all efforts to lure him out of his reclusive state failed. He just sat in the farthest corner of his cave—a sad shadow of himself.

One summer's evening, after returning late from a boat outing on Lake Mead, I checked on Macumba and saw only his beautiful emerald green eyes staring into the night from inside his cave. I could stand it no longer; he was wasting away to nothing. I carefully entered his den, sat on the far side of his cave, and spoke softly to him. His only response was a frightful snarl with saliva dripping down the sides of his fangs. I pretended to ignore him and began to meditate.

After a short time, I first sensed, then heard a movement. Not breaking my meditation, I sat hushed and still, while I felt him moving toward me. I could feel his hot breath and hear his jaws opening. Without opening my eyes, I pushed him off, and he retracted from the touch. At that moment I realized he was coming out of his shell and the moment of truth was *near*. Another ten minutes passed, and I could feel him approaching again. This time I decided to take my chances and not push him away. If he was going to bite me, it might as well happen now because at some point I knew his sorrow would have to surface. Though in a state of meditation, I was acutely aware of the rustling of every piece of straw on the floor. Suddenly I felt a paw on my knee and then something heavy on my legs. I opened my eyes. Macumba had laid his weary head in my lap. A shiver ran through my body.

Macumba had returned to life.

I spent the next few weeks building on this moment. To create a little curiosity and movement around him, I placed Macumba next to Sabu, my older black panther, and Sasha, my spotted leopard. It was in this situation that I detected a touch of jealousy in Macumba—another good sign that he was on his way to recovery.

As when a child realizes that you want him to do something, I could sense a little resentment stirring in Macumba, so I misdirected him and put our relationship on hold. Instead, I placed the emphasis on familiarizing him with Sabu and Sasha and hoped they would form a threesome. That day came sooner than I anticipated. Except for a few snarls and false halfhearted attacks, they slept together every night. Even though Sabu and Sasha were a couple, old Sabu didn't mind sharing his lady with his new friend. Sasha had the least objection. It seemed their lifelong marriage got a healthy new spark—what a fun group.

About a year later Sabu's arthritis made his stage appearances difficult, so against his will I retired him. Macumba had been coming to the theater with me, and I had noticed that he always watched my rehearsals with Sabu and had begun to envy the attention I paid Sabu. Now that I had built up the emotional trust, I knew he was ready for what I call affection conditioning.

As it happened, Macumba not only became a thriving, happy, and affectionate cat but turned out to be a natural for the stage and is the biggest ham of all.

Today, when I hear my friends boast about the qualities and accomplishments of their children and remark upon how the time, devotion, and nurturing have paid off, I nod my head in agreement.

Siegfried

One of the great rewards of our success has been the opportunity we've had to meet so many interesting and famous people. In our private apartment the walls are lined with twenty years of photographs of wonderful after-the-show evenings with some of the greatest performers, royalty, politicians, and dignitaries. It seems so strange to us. Here are people we're in awe of, and *they're* coming backstage to meet *us*.

I would have to say, though, the most memorable meeting was when we turned the tables and went backstage. In this case, however, backstage was at the Vatican, and the dignitary we were going to see was His Holiness Pope John Paul II.

The idea to have an audience with His Holiness all began as a present to my sister, Margot, who is a Franciscan nun who lives in Germany. Her order takes care of very difficult children who come to them after having the most awful childhoods imaginable. Roy had once asked her, "Margot, if you had one wish, what would you wish for?"

"Since childhood, I've dedicated my life to Christ and the church. I would, more than anything, like to make a pilgrimage to the Vatican and meet His Holiness the pope," she answered.

In 1986, after many years, Bernie was able to arrange this meeting through contacts with the White House.

Roy

At the same time I had a little idea about something I wanted to discuss with the pope. It had always been my ultimate goal for the white tigers to live free again in the wilderness. And I figured that the pope and the high lamas could help me achieve that. For there's an area in the Himalayas so remote that it's really nobody's land. It is therefore everybody's land. I felt I couldn't do better than the pope as an ally.

The white tiger seemed very far away when we met up with Margot and her mother superior in Germany. The mother superior had never flown before. She did what first-time travelers often do: She imitated her more experienced companions. So on the plane, after I had ordered a Campari and orange juice, when the flight attendant moved on to the mother superior, she very pleasantly said, "Oh, I'll have the same." Margot, in turn, followed her superior. What they thought they were getting, I'll never know. But the

Eddie Murphy

After our show we always entertain our backstage guests with close-up magic. Besides making a rose bush bloom, the ultimate favorite among our visitors is when we ask them to choose a card from a deck of fifty-two and sign it—the same way as in their checkbooks, of course! Then with Siegfried and Roy handcuffs— a rubber band—we secure the deck. One-Two-Three! The card can be found floating on the ceiling where bedazzled guests soon discover that their names are levitating with the best and the brightest.

His royal Highness, Prince Rainier of Monaco, his son Prince Albert and the prince of show business, Cary Grant.

Dolly Parton

Bob Hope

Don Rickels

Sylvester Stallone

Mr. and Mrs. Kirk Douglas

Julio Iglesias

Robin Williams

Liberace

James Brown

A

B

C

D

E

F

A– A Schwarzenegger, a Kennedy, a Siegfried, a Roy, and the Royal White Tigers of Nevada—seven examples of the American Dream

B– One of Siegfried's inspirations, our everlasting French connection—Charles Aznavour

C– **Vincent Price**
A mystical man and a great actor

D– Whenever we visit someone, we're certain we'll be asked to perform some magic. So when President Bush invited us to the White House, we thought he might suggest that we make the budget deficit disappear.
Sorry, George!

E– President and Mrs. Ronald Reagan sending us on our way to the Vatican to visit Pope John Paul II and to relay their greetings to His Holiness from them and the people of America

F– And just to show we're not politically biased—our favorite Democrat, Jimmy Carter

G– Steven Spielberg's birthday present to his mother was to fly her to Las Vegas to see our show

H– Barbra Streisand

H

G

To Siegfried & Roy,

You brought Fantasia to life right before my eyes. I'm spellbound!

Steven Spielberg
Oct 25, 1990

A

B

C

A– **With Walter Cronkite**
Even as a cub, our Nubian lion, Mombasa, enjoyed being embraced by the power of the media.

B– *"Cats"! "Starlight Express"! "Phantom of the Opera"! What will Andrew Lloyd Webber do next? A musical version of our lives?*

C– **An endangered, but not yet extinct species**
Left to right: Roger Moore, Gregory Peck, Gene Autry, Frank Sinatra, and Steve Wynn

D– **I did it my way, he did it his way— and we drank to it.**

E– **With our breathtaking Lady Elizabeth at Roy's birthday party, October 1991**
Our manager, Bernie Yuman, arranged to have Elizabeth Taylor fly in from Los Angeles as a surprise guest for my birthday party. It was four days before her marriage to Larry Fortensky, the night of her bridal shower, and she had to escape the media by climbing over a neighbor's wall. She arrived on a plane just before midnight, in time to sing "Happy Birthday" at the stroke of twelve. I joined in and soon we were both singing perfectly out of tune—the only interruption was our laughter. After that we reassured each other we would stick to our real professions.

F– *Every year, Muhammad Ali, who's a great friend and magic buff, attends the Desert Magic Seminar that we sponsor for new talent. On this occasion The Greatest was surprised to discover that his magic wasn't just limited to the ring—he, too, could pull rabbits out of a hat!*

G– **Can we talk?**
Joan Rivers—a funny lady and always a helping friend. She assisted us in our TV show and we assisted in hers. But after sawing her in half and deliberately not putting her together again, she was not responsible for what came out of her mouth.

H– **Mr. High Voltage**
Sammy Davis, Jr., was a friend for twenty-five years and when we lost him, some of the lights on the strip went out.
So many warm memories—talking late into the night after his shows and ours; we always drew from his energy. His opening nights were electric. For us he represented the best of Las Vegas.

D

G

E

F

H

Kevin Costner and Oliver Stone

King Carl Gustaf of Sweden visiting the Jungle Palace

The announcement of his request to visit us put our entire household in total chaos. The staff worked fervently around the clock—the king comes, the king comes. An hour before His Majesty's arrival the grounds were given a final check. What a scare! The place was crawling with security—guards were hiding in our 280 palm trees. Suddenly we noticed a shabby old van across the street. How dare someone park that in front of our house! Roy ran to tell the driver to leave and soon got an even greater sense of the responsibility of such a prominent visitor. The van was a camouflage—loaded with electronic devices and more security. We braced ourselves for a strained visit. But like so many aristocrats, His Majesty was charming, even humble. And he didn't even blink when La Donna, the cockatoo, screamed, "Long live Roy!"

Bruce Willis and Demi Moore

An Inspiration to an Inspiration

After one of Liza Minnelli's electrifying performances, I confessed to her that I played her tapes religiously before I went on stage, as her energy stimulated and inspired me. To my surprise, she took my hand and pulled me through the cocktail-sipping crowd to her private chamber. My mind was racing . . . what now?

All alone in a tiny room, what did my favorite girl do? She pulled out a tape recorder and said, "Please, Roy, say the same thing you just told me. That's what gives me the adrenalin to do what I do."

General Norman Schwarzkopf

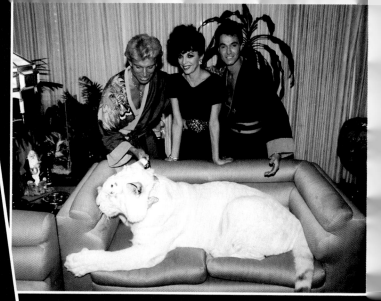

A rare species and beauty of a woman

Why did Joan Collins lock herself in a bathroom after meeting two of the world's most desirable showbiz bachelors?

You probably would have done the same.

After meeting for the first time, tigress Joan and tigress Sitarra argued over who was going to sit on the sofa. When Sitarra stretched out on the actress, Joan's gorgeous legs did the walking. This triggered a playful chase around the sofa, which ended with Joan retreating to the bathroom in fear. A smiling Sitarra returned to the sofa and licked her paws.

Perhaps this is why we were never on Dynasty.

With George Burns
at his ninety-fifth birthday celebration

We were performing the night of George's party. In between shows at the Mirage we raced over to Caesar's Palace.

"George, the good surprise is that we came to the party," announced Roy. "The bad surprise is that I'm going to sing 'Happy Birthday.'"

"Oh, kid, how can you do this me?" asked George, sucking on a cigar for solace.

"If we didn't love and admire you so much we would never subject you to this," Roy explained. And with Roy leading the way, two thousand people sang along. George was touched, but he recovered sufficiently to get the last laugh.

"Kid, you may have a second career after all."

Günther Gebel-Williams—The Lord of the Rings

Roy

I was about ready to give all the passports back and tell them all to go home; I would go alone to Germany with the tigers. But then Siegfried returned, and by that time everyone was feeling a bit better. And off we went to Germany.

Siegfried

We arrived at the Phantasialand celebration. We were treated like heads of state and welcomed by government officials and Richard Burt, the United States ambassador to West Germany. The red carpet was rolled out; the marching band was playing. The German press had heard about the escapade in New York, and that drew even more of a crowd. The best part of all was that SiegRoy and Vegas felt immediately at home in their new surroundings and didn't mind becoming German.

In addition to Phantasialand, another event had been planned. It was June, around the time of my birthday, and the city of Rosenheim had decided to honor the occasion by presenting us with the key to the city. The mayor gave me a huge birthday party at the city hall. Six thousand people—all of whom claimed to know me when I was a boy—showed up, and we were mobbed with requests for autographs and photos. My brother, who still lives in Rosenheim, couldn't believe it. All he could say was: "This is impossible. Bavarians don't do this."

Our crown jewels of nature, peacefully at home in their white habitat

Sharing in the 25th birthday celebration of Phantasialand with our dear friends and long-time supporters, the owners of the European theme park which is home to two of the Siegfried and Roy Royal White Tigers. Above, with Sohni Loeffelhardt, who greeted us and our manager, Bernie Yuman, upon our arrival to film the television special for the anniversary. Below, with co-owner Richard Schmidt, at the press conference heralding the birthday.

Then it was time for the mayor to make the presentation. Just as he was about to begin his speech, he realized he'd forgotten the heavy gold ceremonial necklace worn for all official occasions. So he sent one of his assistants back to his office to retrieve it. A few minutes later, with necklace in hand, the presentation was now ready to begin. But just as the mayor picked it up to place around his neck, Roy—for some reason unknown to me—thought the mayor was giving him the necklace as a present. Thanking him profusely, he tried to take it from the mayor's hands.

Here I was in my hometown, and my partner was trying to run off with the city jewels.

A white-tiger habitat has been created at Phantasialand in Bruhl, Germany. And with the vision of Steve Wynn we created one at the Mirage Hotel so that we could give the public—and schoolchildren, in particular— the opportunity to enjoy and learn about the white tiger free of charge.

It was a very embarrassing moment, to say the least. Thank God the Bavarians have a good sense of humor. But like I say, Murphy's Law.

R*oy*

That's the difference between Siegfried and me. I recall the trip as being really, really fun, challenging and all the rest. We did radio and television shows in Germany. With our entourage and a caravan of suitcases we went to Venice and Paris. It was in Venice that Siegfried discovered the masks and black capes the Venetians wear at their masked balls. He became fascinated by the costumes and took them back to Las Vegas. And that was the evolution of the Siegfried and Roy miracle workers, who walk around the theater in mask and cape, placing stars, hearts, white tiger emblems, and magic dust on people. A lot of good things came out of that visit.

254

I never talked to so many people in my life. Everywhere we went, we were approached for autographs or photos, and I enjoyed every minute of it.

Siegfried

Well, Roy's right. As for the party in Rosenheim, this event was really like my homecoming; emotionally that was far more important than the honor. The way I left my hometown and the way I returned were worlds apart. It was something I had always fantasized—the people of Rosenheim embracing me, for little Siegfried, who had left as "nobody," was now returning as "somebody."

There was only one thing missing: my mother. It was her that I thought most of at this celebration. And I was reminded of the last time I saw her and my final words.

When I was still working on the cruise ship, I took a few days off to visit my parents. My father was ill, and I knew he didn't have long to live. My mother didn't look well either. Though she said nothing, I knew something was wrong. On the day I had to return to the ship, she asked if I would take her to the train station so she could go and visit my sister.

While waiting for the train, she looked up at me and said, "You know, I have only one worry now in my life. I'm not worried about your brother; he has a family and a business. Margot has found her calling and has chosen a life for herself. My only worry is you, Siegfried."

I put my arms around her and gave her a deep embrace. "Ma, you don't have to worry. The time will come when you'll be very proud of me. I promise." That brought a smile to her face, and I knew she understood.

With tears in our eyes, she boarded the train. I waved her off. I stood there until the train was out of sight. Somehow I knew that was the last time I would see her.

I returned to Bremerhaven for the next Atlantic crossing. When I reached New York, there was a telegram waiting for me: My mother had passed away. My father followed her a year later. And though it was hard to accept that I had lost my parents in such rapid succession, I took comfort in knowing that I had made my peace with both of them before they died and I didn't have to carry around with me any unresolved relationships for the rest of my life.

But on this festive day in Rosenheim all I could think was that if my mother could see me now, she would know I had kept my promise.

...imagine sitting in a theater believing that what you see is real. Or if that's to much to swallow, then imagine asking yourself just for a moment if it might be. To be given in the theater the gift of that doubting, of the possibility of miracle! Once a possibility is admitted, the reality hardly matters. To be able to give such a gift...

—MARJORIE KELLOGG,
FROM *HARMONY*

ACT SEVEN

Siegfried

As magicians we have, over the years, met all sorts of people who are involved in the psychic arts. And because of what we do, we also seem to attract these people. People write letters to Roy or to me saying they saw our show and realized at that moment they had known one or both of us in a previous life.

Just before we went to the MGM, we met a Hungarian Gypsy in Puerto Rico. She was an extraordinary woman: During World War II she had survived the Nazi persecution of Gypsies in her country, she had escaped from a plane crash in which there were no other survivors, and she had traveled all over the world. At one point she had lived in Paris and knew people we had known there. She was also a psychic and had been the adviser to King Farouk of Egypt and to European society and royalty. But it wasn't Contessa Gypsy de Markoff's powers that attracted me; I loved to hear the stories of her life.

For me, fortune-telling has always been a form of entertainment, and I indulged in it somewhat when Roy and I did our mind-reading act in the old days. I've always believed that if a soothsayer predicts something for you and it comes true, it's because something has been unlocked in your subconscious that allows it to happen. The fortune-teller's words serve as a catalyst to the realization of your dreams.

In the midst of all my unhappiness at the MGM I had begun to believe we couldn't expand any further in Las Vegas. I decided that after we had finished playing there, we would go back to Europe. The Gypsy came to visit us while we were doing *Hallelujah Hollywood*. I told her my plan, and she couldn't resist reading the tarot cards.

"No, no," she said, "you're not going anywhere. You're staying right in Las Vegas."

"What do you mean?"

"You're going to have your own show here, with your own theater built for you."

Our life is the stage, the stage is our life, and our home is a true expression of our personalities and a gathering place of travels and memories.

Excerpts from our world tour

Excerpts from our world tour

Posing with Japan's highest-ranked Sumo wrestler

When he came to see our show we had to revamp the VIP box—six chairs put together would not accommodate him. A last-minute emergency arose before curtain time. In order to make him more comfortable we

sent our eight-foot-long sofa from our dressing room. Once that dilemma was solved another drama occurred. He came to visit us backstage, laden with presents. But there was one problem; he couldn't get through the set of double doors made for ordinary, humble mortals. What did we do? In

a shot, we had the doors taken off their hinges and removed— a heavy emotional moment in more ways than one.

Day magic on the Orient Express

One evening over dinner we had casually mentioned to our Japanese producer that since childhood we had always dreamed of riding the Orient Express. By sheer coincidence, the legendary train—which now travels between London and Venice—had been airlifted

from London to Japan for a tour of the country. When our producer learned of our wish, he arranged for us to have a private journey on it from Tokyo to Kyoto.

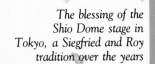

The blessing of the
Shio Dome stage in
Tokyo, a Siegfried and Roy
tradition over the years

With Lynette as guests of
honor at the Japanese premiere
of D. W. Griffith's classic
silent film Intolerance

Our Japanese producer, Dan
Yoshida, invited us to share in
the Foreign Correspondents
Club of Japan's press
conference and luncheon to
announce that our show had
grossed $55 million—which
made it the highest-grossing live
entertainment show in the
history of Japan.

Geisha, Geisha, Geisha

Celebrating our second Japanese birth

Twenty-eight thousand people wrote to Fuji Television to name the new arrivals. These schoolchildren represented the vote of the people and assisted us in officially announcing the names to the public. And the winners were . . .

Ichiban—Japanese for
*   Number One*
Sakura—cherry blossom
Kakkoii—cool

Geisha, Geisha, Geisha

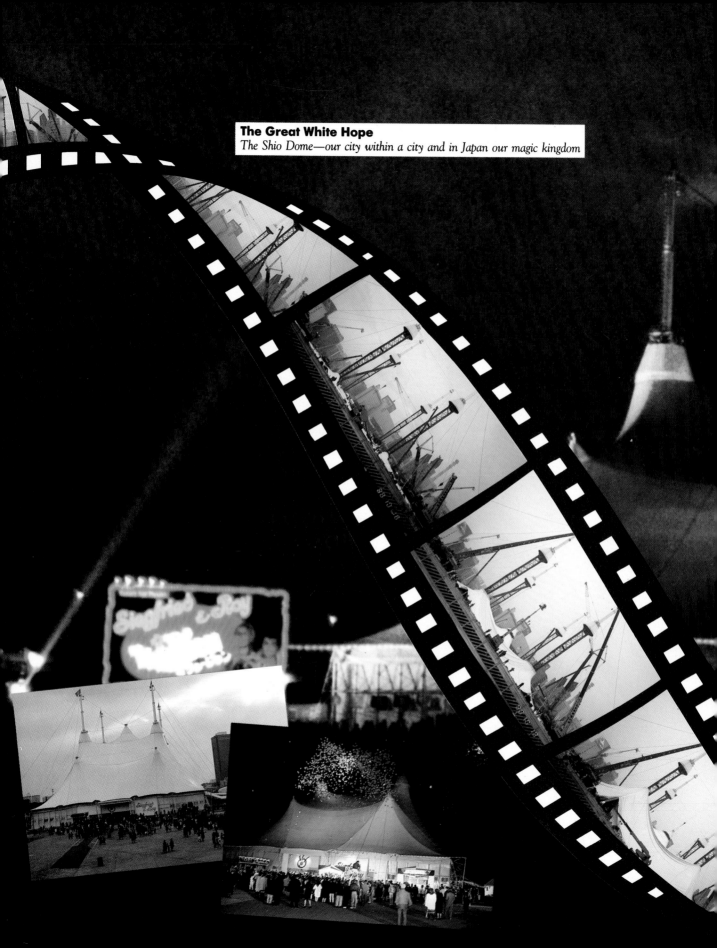

The Great White Hope
The Shio Dome—our city within a city and in Japan our magic kingdom

Kenneth Feld and Bernie Yuman prepare Roy for the inspection and grand tour of our high-tech theater in the heart of Tokyo's Ginza.

ultimate realization of a fantasy for us; it was like a peacock getting an extra feather. Thirty years earlier two German boys had walked off a ship in New York and gone to see the Easter show at Radio City; from that day on it had been our fantasy to play there. And each night when we stood on the Radio City stage, our eyes wandered up to the third row in the balcony, and we still saw those two boys with a big dream looking down on us. I would tell each audience the story, and I couldn't get through it without choking up.

Roy

As always, I couldn't let both of us have the same emotion at the same time. Siegfried thought about yesterday; I had to think about today. So I would go down into the audience, climb on the seats, and embrace people at the end. Of course, the choreographer and director were totally against it. They told me that New Yorkers wouldn't respond; when a show is over, they put their coats on, make a fast exit, and run for a taxi.

I knew from experience that New Yorkers were warmer than that. I went ahead with my plan, and we got a standing ovation every night. Playing at Radio City was my experience of the American Dream come true.

Siegfried

If we had written it ourselves, we wouldn't have been able to write the review we got in *The New York Times*: "For you blasé Gothamites, if you want to see a good effect, go watch the chandelier fall in 'Phantom of the Opera,' but if you want to see the reason for which Radio City Music Hall was built, go see Siegfried and Roy."

And the people came. We broke a fifty-seven-year-old box-office record.

Our show in New York was too big for Broadway, so we went to Radio City Music Hall, but we still had the pleasure of playing Broadway every night on the Kodarama in the middle of Times Square.

Roy

"When you decide to change your show, never change more than fifty percent." That pearl of wisdom was told to us by Liberace. And that was exactly our intention when we began preparing for our show at the Mirage in 1987. We would keep the concept of the story line—good triumphing over evil—and take our greatest hits and give them a new presentation. In addition, we now had twenty-three white tigers, so we wanted to underscore the miracle of these jewels of nature, not with illusion but through sheer presence.

We knew what we didn't want for the Mirage: no conventional backdrops for scenery, no production numbers, no glitzy costumes, no nudity; in short, nothing that was traditional Las Vegas. And we knew what we wanted as well: to create a production that was total magic, from lights to sound to sets, music, and costumes. Everything would depend on everything else.

Siegfried

The magical quality would begin from the minute the audience entered the theater: the lasers, the lighting, the music, the miracle workers. The environment would prepare them for the experience. We wanted the show to be a series of magical moments: the magic of illusions, the magic of nature, and the magic of technology. I didn't want to go out and tell people the great things that Roy and I could do, but to show them the wonderful things that are happening in life. Just open your eyes and look around you. And we hoped that by creating this atmosphere for our audience, we would stimulate their fantasies and make them, if only briefly, delve into their own imaginations.

The show would be more like a Broadway production with a beginning, a middle, and an end. Siegfried and Roy would be emissaries who enter an imaginary world. Through our illusions we would create in almost biblical terms a universe with all the elements of nature materializing. Our magical powers would successfully combat the forces of evil that prevailed in this unknown world. Within this mysterious environment we wanted to create a piece of dramatic scenery that actually functioned, like a monster, a space alien, or a dragon—an idea that had been brewing in our imagination for some time.

Napier's technology and our illusions had to be in sync. In rehearsal the computerized lights, music, and sound were working; they just weren't working with us.

Our staging had never been integrated like this. In the past we had controlled everything. Now, when the dragon raised Roy twenty feet in the air and impaled him, he was at the mercy of modern technology; when he swung on a rope high over the heads of the audience, the computer was running the entire action. It frightened us that in so many situations we were reliant on technology.

And there was reason to be. Once the dragon raised Roy fifty feet in the air, and he went crashing through some of the overhead equipment and, by the grace of God, missed being decapitated by barely a hair. Another time during the slide for life, he went flying out over the showroom and a computer problem sent him slamming against the wall at the back of the theater and then across the showroom at fifty miles per hour, smack into another wall. He was then dragged across the tables and chairs, until he was abruptly deposited on the floor. That wild ride cost him a broken foot and several cracked ribs. We're no strangers to stage accidents—over the years Roy has had his share of torn ligaments, smashed kneecaps, a broken foot and broken fingers more than once, stitches from landing on top of the tables and cutting himself on the glasses and bottles, a few knocked-out teeth here and there—but strangely enough, never even as much as a scratch from any of his animals. We roll with punches; it's just part of the job. But to adjust to the idea that an electronic device is the culprit can make you feel somewhat powerless to do anything to prevent the accident.

Roy

Believe me, that mechanical dragon was harder to train than any tiger. The dragon was, and still is, really like a person with a heart and a soul. The technology enabled it to make all the movements of a human being, which, of course, had to be choreographed and computerized to death. At one point it even had feet. But we couldn't get it to stop walking, and it ended up in the casino one day, so we put wheels on it—with brakes.

John Napier

This show was without a doubt the most difficult thing I've ever done in my life. Everyone's nerves were frayed at the end. I would sum up my experience as unforgettable.

**She walks, she talks,
she has a mind of her own—
Siegfried on stage at the Mirage with
his favorite girl, Mabel**

*Mabel was designed by the French movie, television,
and theatrical producer Christian Fechner,
who's been a source of inspiration for us over the
years. He began his career as a
magician and is still active in the craft. He
attributes a great part of his success in film, TV, and
theater to his application of the principles of
magic. Like us, he feels that magic contains all the
fundamental elements of popular
entertainment. He is, in France, in the same
pantheon that Steven Spielberg and George
Lucas are in America; he uses special effects to make
magic on the grand scale.*

*Rehearsing for our show at the Mirage was a series of dramatic highs
and lows. At one point we were desperately looking for
a moment of comic relief; nothing we attempted seemed appropriate.
One afternoon in the thick of rehearsal we received
a call from someone who said he had a gift to
deliver to us on behalf of Christian Fechner.
It was, of course, our beloved skeleton, Mabel, who
could magically walk on stage twice a night
and provide us with the humor that we needed.
Each night when we hear the roar
of laughter from our audience
we think of Christian Fechner.*

*We respect his boundless creativity,
but more importantly we cherish his friendship.*

And I now look back on it with nostalgia. I've gone to see the show since it opened, and each time I see something that Siegfried, Roy, and I gave birth to together. And I would, with all the agony, do it all over again because it ultimately led to something that I think is going to be regarded as a landmark piece of entertainment.

Roy

Maybe, but before we opened, it felt like we were giving birth to a landmark disaster. I'm certain by the time we had our last rehearsal, which was most traumatic of all, the entire production team was hoping that both Siegfried and I would get impaled by the dragon—for real!

Opening night was, for all involved, heart-stopping. The cast and crew of 164 were petrified; the backstage area, usually humming with hushed, excited chatter on a first night, was oddly silent.

And Siegfried and me? Well, in some ways, not much has changed in all our years together. In retrospect, opening night at the Mirage wasn't that much different from our first professional performance in 1964 at the Astoria Theater in Bremen. Siegfried was having a breakdown, saying, "Why me? Why did you convince me to do this show, Roy? I can't go on." And once again I answered, "Don't worry, Siegfried, everything is going to be perfect. I know we'll succeed." The difference was this time I didn't lock him in the dressing room, I didn't run out for bratwurst and Coca-Cola, and Frau Fritz wasn't there to reassure him.

No, instead, we had Steve Wynn, Kenneth Feld, and Bernie Yuman sweating bullets and praying. If we crashed, we'd be taking a lot of people down with us.

I could see John Napier in the audience, and at every crucial moment when he knew something disastrous could happen, he'd be too terrified to look and he'd throw his hands to his face. At last he saw that we had everything under control, and he sat back like a kid.

We've never savored applause as we did that night. And when we went backstage, we were greeted with a round of claps and cheers from our cast and crew. And we applauded them. After all that worry about survival, we triumphed.

By opening night, though, everyone was burned out. Everyone but us. Which is natural. The struggle, the drama, the emotional torture that go into conceiving a show and putting it together—they are natural for us because the stage is our life and our life is the stage, and we thrive on it.

"Don't call us just magicians or conjurers, storytellers would be just right."

Now we have the show we wanted, the show we always dreamed about. It truly is a realization of thirty years of fantasy, a metaphor for our life and our philosophy. It says, more directly than we could ever have hoped, what we aspire to be for our audience: masters not just of illusion but of human possibility.

Siegfried

Every morning at seven o'clock, as there has been for almost three years, a long line of people winds through the lobby of the Mirage to buy tickets to the most expensive show in town, our show. By ten it's sold out. We play to fifteen hundred people, twice a night, six days a week, forty weeks a year. And all day long people from all walks of life—young and old alike—visit the white tiger habitat that has become a symbol of the Mirage.

Our life is a catalog of new opportunities. We have the largest private collection of tigers in the world—from Bengal to Sumatran, Siberian, white, and snow white—and our menagerie keeps growing. Roy's knowledge and understanding of exotic animals and the success he's achieved in raising them have proved to be an invaluable resource for zoologists. He is now involved in a project with the Cincinnati Zoo to study and learn more about the snow leopard, and to do that, he's raising one, Manchu.

And in 1993, MCA/Universal Cartoon Studios will produce a television series called *Siegfried and Roy, Masters of the Impossible*. Our animated selves will be playing five mornings a week on the Fox TV Network. Using the first letters of the words in the title we've invented an acronym—Sarmoti—that will be the magical word that helps us battle an evil sorceress and protect the fragile world ecology. And, incredibly, the artist Boris Vallejo is a design consultant on the show.

We have achieved all the success we could ever hope for, and more, and when I look back, I feel as if my whole life has been magic. How did I get so far? How did all this happen? Logical answers—talent, hard work, discipline, and unwavering commitment—don't diminish the wonder of it all. I'm still stunned.

Because I can never get used to being who I've become, inside I am still Siegfried out of Rosenheim, still doubting myself, still wondering if I can live up to each challenge. When we signed our megamillion-dollar contract with the Mirage, everyone thought I would jump for joy. But inside I felt smaller and smaller. The bigger the contract, the greater the pressure.

Roy

And thank God for pressure. It keeps me in check. For me fame and success are still fragile, intangible rewards that have no certainty, as they should be. When you accept the rewards, you also have to understand that they will last only as long as you're willing to give. The moment you start to cheat your audience, you're history.

That's why, in our minds, we've never had a perfect show. There's always something that can be better. There's always a light cue or a sound effect or a dancer's costume that's not right.

The ultimate goal every single night for us is to satisfy our audience. When we look out at the end of a show and see fifteen hundred people with wonder and happiness in their eyes, we get something, too: It is from the people we've pleased that we derive our energy and inspiration.

Siegfried

You could say we've never grown up. We still dream as children do, and we want to bring out the children in people, to encourage them to dream as they did when they were children. We've seen enough of life to know that the older you get, the more your dreams get pushed down and buried, and a human being without fantasy, without dreams, is nothing.

We also know that every person has a secret chamber. We want to be the medium for those private fantasies. Through us, maybe our audience can dream. To be able to generate dreams for thousands of people at a time—that is our ultimate pleasure.

Roy

Once again that takes us back to the beginning, to the hard years, when dreams were all we had. And I remember, in those years of struggle, that I often went to Rosenheim with Siegfried to visit his mother. She never saw us perform, so I painted the colors for her of how the spotlight hit Siegfried, and how the drumroll of the three-piece orchestra played for him, and how he entered in his tuxedo with his top hat, cape, white gloves, and cane—and how he gave people pleasure. And he, who was nobody at the time, I assured her, was someone great and would someday be recognized for his gift.

And to my mother and my aunt Paula, who had given me their blessing but still worried about my future, I described our show as I imagined it in my head. I told each of them stories about me astride a tigress, floating in midair on a shimmering silver globe over the heads of the audience. Our name were in lights, and the audience always applauded us wildly.

In two towns I gave our loved ones the fantasies they could never hope to see come true. Perhaps it was because of them that I reached deep into what really was the future.

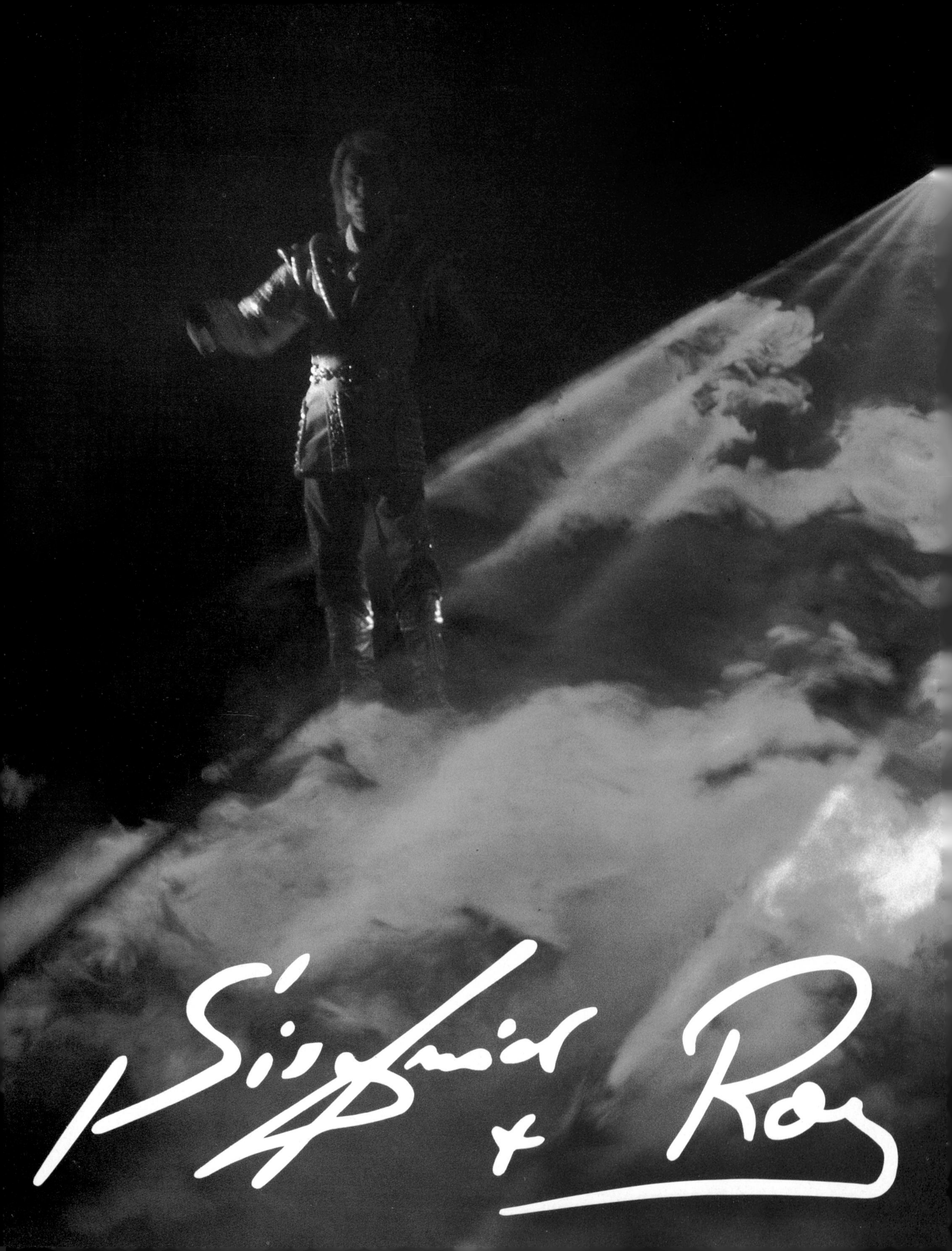

Acknowledgments

The experience of writing a book led us into a new medium of expression and challenged us to see things not just visually but through words. To those who have made a contribution to this project, our gratitude:

- at William Morrow, we thank Howard Kaminsky, whose warmth, wit, and intelligence finally gave us the courage to put our vision on paper, and our editor, Adrian Zackheim, who encouraged us to do what we wanted and meant it;
- our designer, Michael Mendelsohn, who created a book as visually exciting as our show;
- our manager, Bernie Yuman, whose passion, help, and judgment—he says he operates on the "unilateral lack of objectivity that this is the greatest theatrical experience in the history of mankind"—was invaluable during the writing and editing process;
- and our co-writer, Annette Tapert, who reminded us that truth was more magical than fiction.

Lauren Wilder,
our personal photographer

We would like to thank the following photographers whose work appears in this book:

Lauren Wilder, our personal photographer, who has documented us and our family of animals for more than a decade and made sure that our lives were captured in 8 × 10 glossies; Bruce Weber for a "new look"; Greg Gorman for capturing the moment; Wolfgang Wergin for his participation and love for animals; Gerhard Komar, who did our first stage photos in Germany thirty years ago; Neil Leifer for putting our image—life-size—in New York's Times Square; Howard Bingham, one of the best in the business and a true gentleman; Volker Hinz of *Der Stern* magazine; Benedict Hilliard, Chris Kalis, and Mark Seliger; and Karsh of Ottawa for kind permission to reprint his photograph of Irvin Feld; Michael Montfort; Horst Ossinger; Bernd Kollmann; Robert Scott Hooper.

Special thanks to:

The Las Vegas News Bureau for constant community coverage; The Las Vegas *Sun* newspaper and the Greenspuns; The *Review-Journal* newspaper; The German media for keeping our image alive; and to Pro-Processing and Cashman photographers for printing thousands of our photos.

Our world is full of people who have, over the years, supported our career. We would like to thank our families, our friends, and our team of loyal associates. All of you have touched our lives and helped us reach our dreams. A very deep bow to:

Roy's family
- my mother, Johanna, whose love, encouragement, and passion made all of this possible;
- Aunt Paula, who was like a mother to me. Her wisdom still prevails. My love and prayers are with you every day of my life—plus one;
- Emma and Ludwig Behrens for being there in the beginning; and my brothers, Alfred, Manfred, and Werner, whose tough training made their kid brother fit for life.

Siegfried's family
- in memory of my parents, Marin and Maria Fischbacher, whose love—though often hidden, in true Bavarian fashion, under a hard shell—made me strong and capable;
- my brother Marinus, his wife, Hertel, and their children, Marinus, Jr., Sylvia, Barbel, Karen, and the entire Fischbacher clan;
- and Margot, Sister Dolores, whose gift of spiritualism and insight has helped me to reconcile with the past.

We've never forgotten those who helped us enormously in the early days of our career. Our appreciation to:
- Captain Vollmer, Captain Rossinger and the Nord German Lloyd;
- Paul Lepach and Frau Herzog for providing our first stage and a taste of the New World;
- Pfarrer John Stradler for encouragement, with thanks from all of us, Kastenauer;
- Marianne Knief, who helped in her way to give us the break she never got;
- and Weberei Weinberger, for a learning experience in dexterity.

To our extended family, who have contributed to making our lives easier and are always there when it's important: Nancy Bohnett, Joey Brown, John Brown, Lynette Chappell, Bettina D'Ettore, Bob Downey, Fay Gordon, Corliss Holiday, Paul Kelsey, Mia Münzell, Annee Noona, Dennie Pasion (our personal hair stylist, who's had the strength to live through twenty-eight different image changes), Dieter Pohl, Bettina Saade, Martha and Magnus Wilhelm, Marianne Young, Sandy Peters, and Sofie Reckelwell.

To the members of our team, for their tireless energy and devotion in all aspects of our career.

Front row: Kenneth Feld (center), producer of "Siegfried and Roy at the Mirage," and our manager, Bernie Yuman (right). Back row: (left to right) Mark Ferrario, Jerry Sowalsky, John O'Reilly, our counsel, and Harvey Gettleson, our business manager.

313

Associates and Friends

Our heartfelt appreciation to the entire Feld organization: the late, great Irvin Feld, Kenneth Feld, Bonnie Feld, and daughters Nicole, Alana, and Juliette, Allen Bloom, Chuck Smith, Jerry Sowalsky, and Julian Read and the Read-Poland Associates.

For their close guidance through the legal aspects of our lives: John O'Reilly, Mark Ferriaro, Ed Lubbers, and Phyllis Norquay. By the way, we would still like to know who establishes the property boundaries. We're certain we have an additional foot on the boundary line and land.

Our sincere thanks to our animal support team— Dr. Mike Simon, DVM, Dr. Lanny Cornell, DVM, Dr. Greenwood, DVM, Ellen de Rosa, Baines and Kay Simpson, Roy Bailey, Pieter Van Boorst, and Mark Hoffman.

- To Bill Whitten, who keeps us fashionable without being "in fashion."
- To Kathy "Turkey" Reese, the best dresser Roy has ever had.
- To Keith Brooks for his support and devotion as Siegfried's dresser.

To all professional and amateur magicians and magic clubs and associations around the world for their contribution to our wonderful art form—MAGIC

Mr. Richard Aamot and Rosemarie Hughey, our support team at the Siegfried and Roy Production office. Their tireless efforts and enthusiasm were crucial to the completion of our book. And they're still looking for photo negatives from 1951.

To Pamela Allen, Bernie Yuman's right arm at SAY Entertainment. Her continual dedication and contribution to this enterprise make her an invaluable and indispensable associate. To Hershel Pearl for his unwavering loyalty and contribution.

To Dr. Martin Dinnes, DVM, who is totally responsible for our magnificent animal family from birth to adulthood—a lifetime commitment, not to mention many shared gray hairs during trying times.

- To Mr. Edward J. Maruska, who shares our goal of the perpetuation of the white tiger and whom, quite simply, we are immensely grateful to know.
- To the Zoological Society of Cincinnati for its participation in the preservation of the white tiger.
- To the memory of the Maharaja of Rewa, who made the preservation of the white tiger possible.
- To the Maharaja of Baroda, for his shared involvement in protecting this endangered species.
- To Sohni Löffelhardt and Richard Schmidt, whose foresight in presenting our white tigers at Phantasialand in Bruhl in an educational exchange program with us has made it possible for the people of Germany to enjoy and learn about this rare species.

Our sincere love and appreciation to the Royal White Tiger team:

- Lynette Chappell, whose inner beauty is possibly even greater than her outside, who is our extended arm, archangel, Evil Queen, and whose care for all of us is beyond words;
- The keepers of our Noah's Ark. They share our dreams and care daily for all our animals. Their devotion and commitment astound us: George Diesko, Thomas Maple, John Molnar, Toney Mitchell, Kathy Gard, Buzz Martin, and Monique Bickell—thank you.

George Diesko

Thamas Maple

Toney Mitchell

John Molnar

Kathy Gard

Martin "Buzz" Busby

Monique Bickel

To Steve Wynn and the Mirage staff, our cast and crew at the Mirage, whose dedication and support make it happen nightly. And to the thousands of devoted production crew and cast members over the years—to all of you—we thrive on your support.

To all the stars we've been fortunate to meet during our career, to those who have seen our show, visited with us, inspired us, and become our friends—we thank you.

We would also like to thank everyone on the planet who has accepted our gift of dreams, entertainment, fantasy, and the preservation and perpetuation of the white tiger. It is through our audience that we have learned to experience the true joy of living our dreams. We thank you.

To our animals, for making better people of us.

In a career that has spanned three decades, it is inevitable that there are some people we've forgotten to mention. Anyone we've missed will be recognized in the next book. For there is still so much left to say. But as entertainers, we know that one of the elements of success is to always leave your audience wanting more. Believe us when we say . . . you haven't read anything yet . . .

Look for the magic
that is around you.

In nature, plants, flowers,
and all the animals that
share this planet with us.

Look for it —
and let it enlighten
your heart and your life.

Until we meet again,
auf wiedersehen.

INDEX